CHICAGO

in

50 OBJECTS

CHICAGO

in

50 OBJECTS

JOSEPH GUSTAITIS

THE
History
PRESS

Published by The History Press
Charleston, SC
www.historypress.com

First published 2021

Manufactured in the United States

ISBN 9781467146753

Library of Congress Control Number: 2020948445

To Mary Elizabeth

CONTENTS

CONTENTS

INTRODUCTION

History is written in small things just as much as large ones. Historians of the Middle Ages tell us the adoption of the stirrup was key to putting Europe on the path to world power. The Chinese invention of the compass opened up the entire globe to those who were willing to explore it, and the invention of eyeglasses in thirteenth-century Italy enabled adventurers to read the maps. And where would modern technology be if Alessandro Volta had not developed the electric battery?

When tourists arrive in a city for the first time, they want to see the "historic" sights—the Colosseum in Rome, the Tower of London, the Acropolis in Athens. In Chicago, some sightseeing possibilities include the Water Tower, Hull-House, the Pullman National Monument, Prairie Avenue and the Wrigley Building, just to mention a few. But where are the Chicago equivalents of the stirrup and the compass? They are in many places, actually. The following pages attempt to shed light on some important aspects of the history of the Windy City by illustrating and explaining some objects that are ostensibly humble but have cultural significance. Together, it is hoped they will confirm the wisdom of someone who really knew the value of close inspection, Sherlock Holmes, who said, "It has long been an axiom of mine that the little things are infinitely the most important."

Theoretically, an object can be almost anything. One dictionary definition of *object* is "something material that can be perceived by the senses." In that regard, the moon would be an object, as would a grain of sand, which is an object, according to William Blake, in which we can "see the world." A sentient being, however, probably would not be an object—after all, people resent being viewed as objects, and they probably wouldn't want their pets to be seen that way either.

I wish I could claim to have invented the concept of writing a history through objects, but the practice began in 2010, when the BBC and the British Museum came up with a radio series and an accompanying book, *A History of the World in 100 Objects*. Then came enough sequels to give birth to a genre nicknamed HIAHO (history in a hundred objects). There was *The First World War in 100 Objects*, *A History of Football in 100 Objects* and several more—even *A History of the Future in 100 Objects*. Then the necessity of "100" was dropped and along came *The Islamic World: A History in Objects, China: A History in Objects* and *A History of Intellectual Property in 50 Objects*. When the genre came to America, publishers brought out *The Smithsonian's History of America in 101 Objects*, *A History of New York in 101 Objects*, *A Story of Maine in 112 Objects*, *Apollo to the Moon: A History in 50 Objects* and *A History of Video Games in 64 Objects*. It was time for Chicago to join the list.

These books define objects in different ways, according to their purpose. *The Smithsonian's History of America in 101 Objects* includes the bald eagle and Andrew Carnegie's mansion, and among the items in *A History of New York in 101 Objects* are Johnny Carson and the Cross Bronx Expressway. For the purposes of this book, however, I adopted a more limited definition of *object*. For example, a building is an object, but to tell the history of Chicago by means of its buildings is to write a history of Chicago architecture—and several fine ones already exist. Similarly, I excluded works of art and representation, such as paintings, posters, picture postcards and photographs, as I did not want to create an illustrated history of the Windy City (there are books that do that, too). I also preferred to feature objects that are, for the most part, small enough to be picked up—they are "collectibles."

The process of selecting objects began with the timeline of Chicago history—that is, pivotal events and people were identified before finding an object that might represent them. However, certain objects are closely identified with Chicago's cultural identity more than with its history per se—the Chicago hot dog and the Chicago blues, for example—which meant not everything was linked to a particular event or person. Discovering overlooked or neglected objects can lead to discovering overlooked or neglected people—people who played fascinating roles in Chicago's history. Among those to be found in this book are abolitionist John Jones, architect W.W. Boyington, trader Benjamin "Old Hutch" Hutchinson, musicians Theodore Thomas and James Palao, actor Bryant Washburn, designer Abel Faidy, gangster Fred "Killer" Burke, forensic medicine pioneer Frances Glessner, radio producer Irna Phillips, pizza entrepreneur Ike Sewell and physicians Daniel Hale Williams and Bernard Fantus.

Some of the objects in this book are unique or so rare it would be difficult to put a price on them. They belong in museums, which is where they are. Others, however, are hardly valuable at all in the sense of being investment-worthy; similar objects can be found at garage sales, flea markets and online. This was a deliberate choice, too, for it was my intention to demonstrate that a great many people can afford to build a personal collection of Chicago memorabilia. In fact, acquiring Chicago objects can be both educational and a great deal of fun.

1.

POTAWATOMI WAR CLUB

The first European to see what is now Chicago was probably a French trader. When the Jesuit missionary Jacques Marquette and the explorer Louis Joliet arrived in 1673, they came across two other Frenchmen—Pierre Moreau and one whom we know only as "the Surgeon." When René-Robert Cavelier, Sieur de La Salle, who explored the North American interior in 1682, described the place, he spelled it "Chegagou." The name comes from a plant the Natives called *shikaakwa*. These plants have often been called "wild onions," but most call them the *allium tricoccum*, or ramp. It's said the plants gave the area a pungent smell. Ramps have become so trendy with foodies that, in the early spring, flocks of them tramp through Chicago-area woods uprooting them—so many that some scientists fear they will one day disappear from the land to which they gave their name.

The Native peoples who lived in the Great Lakes region settled in villages and practiced agriculture, but tribal migrations were common. The first Native American people we know who lived in the Chicago area were the Illiniwek, or Illinois, who were displaced by Iroquois tribes that invaded from the east and south. The Miami then settled at the southern end of Lake Michigan, as did the Ho-Chunk, Menominee and Mesquakie, but the most numerous and most remembered were the Potawatomi, or, as they called themselves, "Keepers of the Fire," who were in the Chicago region as early as the 1690s. Tribal identities were fluid but became less so on the arrival of Europeans, when the natives organized themselves into "nations." As this war club indicates, the Native Americans who once lived in the region were

Potawatomi War Club. *Chicago History Museum, ICHi-064722.*

not always the pacifistic hoers of corn and hunters of deer of romantic myth; they were combatants who were often engaged in grim warfare—both with other tribes and with European colonists. The Jesuit missionary Claude Allouez used the word "warlike" to describe the Potawatomi.

What Europeans wanted most from North America was fur, and the indigenous tribes engaged in fur trading with them, especially the French. Many French traders married Native women; their children were known as Métis. The Métis proved to be helpful translators and several played roles in early Chicago, which, at first, had a decidedly French quality. As the British and French warred over North America, the tribes were caught up in the conflict, taking sides with one or the other until the newly independent Americans replaced the British as encroachers on Native territory. The British had, in 1763, agreed, in principle, to remain east of the Appalachians, but the Americans saw the Midwest as a frontier to be settled. Under the Northwest Ordinance of 1787, Congress made plans to divide the Northwest Territory into "not less than three nor more than five states." Eventually, this territory became Ohio, Michigan, Indiana, Illinois, Wisconsin and part of Minnesota. The Native peoples resisted incursion, but a defeat at the Battle of Fallen Timbers in 1794 led to the 1795 Treaty of Greenville, in which the tribes ceded most of the

NAH - SHAW - A - GAA **OR THE WHITE DOG'S SON**

Pottawatomie Chief

Taken at Green Bay treaty 1827 by J.O. Lewis —

Potawatomi chief Nah-Shaw-a-Gaa (1827). *Smithsonian American Art Museum, gift of H. Lyman Sayen to his nation.*

state of Ohio to the United States. The following years saw a succession of battles, treaties and the handing over of more and more land as the settlers pushed west. The most determined struggle was organized by the Shawnee chief Tecumseh and his brother Tenskwatawa, who was known as "the Prophet"; they visited Chicago in 1810 to enlist the Potawatomi in the cause. However, the next year, their resistance was quashed at the Battle of Tippecanoe.

During the American Revolution, the Potawatomi took the side of the rebels, but when the U.S. Army constructed Fort Dearborn at what is now the intersection of Michigan Avenue and Wacker Drive in 1803, relations soured, and when the United States went to war with Britain in 1812, the Potawatomi saw an alliance with the British as their best chance to oust the Americans. U.S. general William Hull recognized that Fort Dearborn could not be defended and ordered its evacuation. When the soldiers and their families departed on August 15, 1812, Potawatomi warriors attacked the column, killing about fifty Americans and taking most of the others captive. This was the legendary Fort Dearborn "Massacre" (historians now prefer "Battle"). The captives were eventually ransomed.

Between 1816 and 1833, the Potawatomi were induced to participate in no fewer than thirty treaties, in which they ceded more and more territory. In 1833, the final pact was concluded, and the Potawatomi gave up their remaining land in Illinois. At the concluding ceremony in Chicago in 1835, five hundred painted warriors staged a final ritual war dance, and then the tribe began its "Trail of Death" trek to the lands west of the Mississippi. Potawatomi chief Aptakisic presented this war club to a settler named Stephen F. Gale.

Many today imagine the Potawatomi to be long gone, but they remain. The 1833 treaty permitted a few to relocate to Michigan, and a tribal leader named Leopold Pokagon led a group to Silver Creek Township. Others went elsewhere in Michigan, and some went to Wisconsin. The Pokagon Band of Potawatomi today is a federally recognized Native American tribe, with a community center in Dowagiac, Michigan, which is also the site of one of the casinos the tribe operates. In 2019, a group of Potawatomi linguists published an 8,500-word Potawatomi-English dictionary. It was published just in time; only about ten fluent speakers of the language were still alive at the time, and all were over the age of seventy. Fans of the Lone Ranger will be interested to know *kibmosabe* means "take a quick look."

2.

MARK BEAUBIEN'S FIDDLE

The first acknowledged non-Native inhabitant of Chicago was a Black man—Jean Baptiste Pointe DuSable, as his name is normally spelled. (However, diligent historians—most notably early Chicago specialist John F. Swenson—have insisted the correct form is Jean Baptiste Point de Sable. They are almost certainly correct, but "Pointe DuSable" appears in so many places, it's unlikely that any revision is possible at this late date.) His heritage was mixed West African and French, and although it's often reported that he was born in Haiti or on another Caribbean island, historians don't really know, nor do they know the year. In 1778, he married a Potawatomi woman named Catherine (Kitihawa), and about seven years later, he settled in Chicago, where he owned a farm. His farm prospered, but he sold it in 1800 and moved west. It's been suggested the racial prejudice of the incoming American settlers spurred his departure and he preferred to live among the Potawatomi and traders he knew best.

DuSable sold his farm to Jean La Lime, who, in turn, sold it William Burnett. In 1804, Burnett sold it to John Kinzie, who has become known as "the father of Chicago." Kinzie (1763–1828) was a silversmith and trader who spoke several Native languages. He had a violent temper, and in 1812, he had a fight with La Lime and killed him with a knife. He married twice and had eight children, the last of whom died in 1887. His daughter-in-law Juliette Kinzie wrote *Wau-bun: The "Early Day" in the North-West* (1856), a priceless document of Chicago's early days.

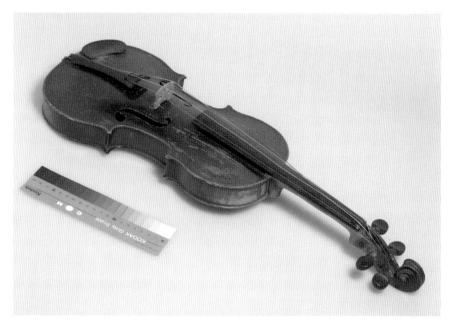

Mark Beaubien's fiddle. *Chicago History Museum, ICHi-040648.*

Perhaps it was the excitement of building a city from nothing or seizing the opportunities of the frontier, but after Kinzie, the little settlement attracted a colorful group of characters. One was Gurdon S. Hubbard (1802–1886), who arrived in 1818. He was initially a fur trader and well acquainted with Native Americans, who nicknamed him "Pa-pa-ma-ta-be," or "Swift Walker," after he reportedly hiked seventy-five miles in one night. Hubbard became known as Chicago's "most useful" inhabitant and was involved in the construction of the Illinois & Michigan Canal and the founding of the Board of Trade. He sold life insurance, was elected alderman, ran passenger ships, built a packing plant and bought the city's first fire engine. He also wrote an eight-hundred-page autobiography, but it was, alas, destroyed in the Chicago Fire, along with nearly all his possessions. Mark Beaubien (1800–1881) came in 1826 from Detroit with his wife and children. He bought a log cabin from Kinzie and turned it into an inn and lodging house located at the south end of Wolf Point. In 1829, he built the Eagle Exchange Tavern (later renamed the Sauganash Hotel), and there, the affable innkeeper would entertain patrons with fiddle music. He once said, "I keep the tavern like Hell, and I play the fiddle like the devil." The instrument seen here is a remarkable survivor of Chicago's infancy. According to the Chicago History Museum, around 1860, Beaubien gave the fiddle to his nephew Louis Mathieu, and it was eventually passed down to Mathieu's great-granddaughter, who donated it to the museum in 1980. Similar to Hubbard in the breadth of his activities was William Butler Ogden (1805–1877), whom the French historian Francois Guizot once called "the representative American," adding, "He built and owns Chicago." Ogden was a crack shot, played the piano and was one of the greatest talkers of the day. He married (for the first time) at the age of seventy. Ogden arrived in Chicago in 1835 as the director of the American Land Company, and only two years later, he was elected the first mayor (Chicago was incorporated as a town in 1833 and as a city in 1837). He laid out streets, commissioned maps, ignited a legendary real estate boom and was instrumental in making Chicago the nation's railroad capital. Then there was "Long John" Wentworth (1815–1888), whose height was reportedly six feet eleven inches (he weighed three hundred pounds). He settled in Chicago in 1836. His purchase of a newspaper gave him considerable influence; he was twice elected mayor and served several terms as a congressman. His gruff manner is illustrated by his famous quotation, "You damned fools. You can either vote for me for mayor or you can go to hell." A keen abolitionist, he was an early member of the Republican Party and backed Lincoln for president in 1860.

Chicago was so young and grew so fast that it's surprising to realize that some of its pioneers lived long enough to see the city become unrecognizable—one of the major cities of the world. When Beaubien arrived, Chicago had comprised about fourteen houses and, at most, one hundred inhabitants—basically a fort and a trading post on a marshy plain. When Long John Wentworth died, the city had a population of about a million people, was the fastest-growing city in history and was a manufacturing, retail and railroading colossus. In 1874, a group of "old settlers" began holding an annual picnic, a tradition that lasted well into the twentieth century. The 1913 picnic, for example, featured two pioneers—John J. O'Neil and Catherine Clark—who had come to Chicago in 1838. Five years later, a reporter interviewed an old settler named C.F. Periolat, who had been living in Chicago for seventy-nine years and remembered when the water pipes were oak logs with four-inch holes bored into them. He said he used to go hunting on Van Buren Street and would get five cents for a mink hide. At the time he was interviewed, he marveled, "A mink of the same class brings ten dollars."

3.

McCORMICK REAPER CENTENNIAL MEDAL

Give us this day our daily bread." This well-known prayer is a reminder of how fundamental bread has been in history. And few others have done more to help us earn "our daily bread" than Cyrus McCormick of Chicago.

In the early nineteenth century, many inventors were attempting to create a machine that would cut, gather and bind sheaves of wheat. One of these inventors was Robert McCormick Jr. (1780–1846), a steadfast experimenter who labored over the device for some two decades. He succeeded in contriving an apparatus that cut grain, but he couldn't solve the problem of how to mechanically gather it, leaving that challenge to his son Cyrus. Cyrus McCormick was born on February 15, 1809, and grew up on the prosperous family farm in Rockbridge County, Virginia. (Today, it's a museum.) In a 1909 biography of McCormick, Herbert Newton Casson explained that no fewer than *seven* hurdles had to be overcome:

1) The reaper had to separate the grain that was cut from what was left standing.
2) The cutting knife had to simultaneously have two motions— forward and sideways.
3) The grain had to be held upright while being cut.
4) The fallen grain had to be lifted and straightened.
5) The cut grain needed a platform to fall on.

6) The machine had to be *pulled* by horses, not *pushed*, as McCormick's father's machine had been.

7) The reaper had to be built "upon one big *driving-wheel*, which carried the weight and operated the reel and cutting-blade."

By 1831, McCormick had solved all of these problems. A year later, he gave a public exhibition, and a local academic exclaimed, "This machine is worth a hundred thousand dollars!" In 1931, the International Harvester Company issued a series of medals, one of which is shown here, to commemorate the centennial of the invention of the reaper. The coins have an image of Cyrus Hall McCormick on one side, and on the other, they have an image of the reaper based on a painting by N.C. Wyeth.

When McCormick patented his reaper in 1834, about four dozen inventors had already done the same, but none of their machines could do all his did. McCormick's major rival was the American Obed Hussey, who patented a reaper a year before McCormick but was slow to market it. However, because Hussey's first public demonstration was in 1833, a year after McCormick's, McCormick insisted he deserved priority. For years, McCormick and Hussey waged fights over patents, but in several head-to-head contests, McCormick's machine prevailed. Also, McCormick's entrepreneurial skills were greater, and by 1858, Hussey was out of the business. By 1840, McCormick had solved one final problem—cutting *wet* grain. The reapers began to sell— seven in 1842, twenty-nine in 1843, fifty in 1844. McCormick didn't just invent a reaper, he invented the business of manufacturing and selling them.

McCormick reaper Centennial Medal. *Author's collection.*

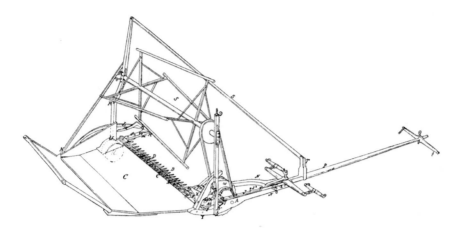

McCormick reaper. *Wikimedia Commons.*

He was a large purchaser of advertising, he let farmers buy on credit and his idea of giving the buyer a money-back guarantee was revolutionary.

As settlers flocked westward and reaper orders began pouring in from the Midwest, McCormick recognized Virginia was no longer an ideal base of operations. To ship reapers to the prairie states, he had to send them by canal to Richmond, transfer them to boats on the James River, send them by sea to New Orleans, and, finally, ship them up the Mississippi River. He canvassed the Midwest, seeking a location near the prairies that was well-served by railroads and on a Great Lake. Chicago still wasn't much, but it fulfilled those requirements, and in 1847, McCormick purchased land on the north side of the Chicago River, built a factory and invited his brothers, Leander and William, to join him. In his first year, McCormick sold five hundred reapers. After the machine proved to be a sensation at the great London Exposition of 1851, he captured the European market. By 1860, he was employing 120 workers, and ten years later, he was selling ten thousand reapers annually.

In its McCormick obituary, the *Chicago Tribune* said he was "mistaken in some of his views," adding, "His Virginia birth and early associations and environments made him a Democrat of strong convictions and yet of conservative tendencies, which increased with age." The newspaper was referring to McCormick's flirtation with politics during the Civil War. He was skeptical of abolition and was identified as part of the "Copperhead" faction of the Democratic Party, which opposed the war and advocated for a negotiated settlement with the Confederacy. The McCormick family farm had owned nine slaves—one of them, Jo Anderson, even helped design the reaper. In a 1931 biography of his grandfather, Cyrus McCormick III wrote, "Jo Anderson deserves honor as the man who worked beside him in the building of the reaper. Jo Anderson was a slave, a general farm laborer, and a friend." McCormick was grateful to Anderson. Well before the Civil War, he gave Anderson his freedom and a cabin, and he regularly wrote him letters from Chicago.

The Great Chicago Fire of 1871 reduced the reaper factory to ashes. McCormick asked his wife, Nettie, who also had an astute business sense, for advice. When she told him to rebuild, his spirits lifted, and he quickly collected as much cash as he could from his company representatives in other cities. The new factory was located on the South Branch of the Chicago River. By the time McCormick died in 1884, it was turning out fifty thousand reapers a year. In the early twentieth century, the McCormick Harvesting Machine Company merged with several other firms to form the International Harvester Company.

In 1820, 72 percent of the American workforce, according to the Census Bureau, was engaged in "farm occupations." Today, less than 2 percent of Americans work in this industry. The McCormick reaper had much to do with this reduction.

4.

CHICAGO BOARD OF TRADE NECKTIE

This colorful piece of neckwear was clearly made to appeal to the traders in the pit of the Chicago Board of Trade (CBOT), who look like a happy bunch here. The octagonal-shaped pit (eventually there were thirty) was the symbol of the CBOT, so the famous author Frank Norris wrote a novel about it—*The Pit* (1903). He wrote of "some great, some restless force…that held the tide of the streets within its grip, alternately drawing it in and throwing it forth. Within there, a great whirlpool, a pit of roaring waters spun and thundered, sucking in the life tides of the city, sucking them in as into the mouth of some tremendous cloaca, the maw of some colossal sewer; then vomiting them forth again, spewing them up and out, only to catch them in the return eddy and suck them in afresh."

In the mid-nineteenth century, the Midwestern prairies were being plowed under for farmland, and a web of railroads centered on Chicago, which made it convenient for farmers to ship their products there to be bought, stored and delivered. Wheat was then being shipped in bulk, not by the bag, and the city had a dozen giant steam-powered grain elevators and could process more grain than any city in the world (a million bushels in 1845). The CBOT was created in 1848 to rationalize the shipping, selling and storing process, and within a few years, it had introduced a grading system for wheat that sorted incoming grain and stored it according to condition and purity. This discouraged farmers from selling adulterated grain and guaranteed quality to purchasers.

Chicago Board of Trade necktie. *Author's collection.*

The CBOT also took on the crucial function of "risk management." Because the gathering of grain occurred in a brief span of time, it was abundant in harvest season, making prices low. Later, as grain stocks diminished, prices rose. Arlene Michlin Bronstein, in her book *My Word Is My Bond: Voices from Inside the Chicago Board of Trade*, quoted a veteran trader: "So, the idea of the Board of Trade was that here was a way for the grain to not depress the price at harvest time. You could sell your grain forward and have a contract for it and extend it during the course of the entire year. There also wouldn't be implicit shortages or much higher prices later in the year." This is the system of "futures" for which the CBOT set official rules in 1865. Futures made it possible for a seller of grain to promise its delivery to a buyer at a certain future date (a "futures contract")—the grain didn't have to change hands at the time it was sold. The owner of contracts could, in turn, use them as security for loans or sell them, which opened up a market for speculators. As historian William Cronon explained in *Nature's Metropolis: Chicago and the Great West*, "By promising to deliver ten thousand bushels of wheat at seventy cents a bushel by the end of June, for instance, one could make $500 if the price of wheat was actually only sixty-five cents at the time,

The Pit at the Chicago Board of Trade. *Library of Congress.*

since the buyer had contracted to pay seventy cents whatever the market price." And once the new technology of the telegraph made it possible to instantly report price fluctuations across the country, nationwide speculation became viable.

Long after the organization's founding, farmers and consumers viewed the CBOT's speculation with skepticism. Much of its history was marked by the high-profile activities of flamboyant speculators, some of whom tried to "corner the market," which led to government inquiries and court cases. The most famous trader was Benjamin Hutchinson, ("all legs and nose, with the complexion of liver sausage and weighing only a hundred pounds") who, in 1888, engineered a corner that drove the price of wheat from $0.90 a bushel to $1.60. "Old Hutch" finally went bust and sold his seat on the board for $900. In the late nineteenth century, populists attacked the activities of the CBOT as out-and-out gambling that hurt ordinary people. What looked particularly fishy was that only a tiny number of futures contracts actually resulted in the delivery of grain to the purchaser. It took a Supreme Court case, *Chicago Board of Trade v. Christie Grain & Stock Co.* (1905), to finally affirm the legality of futures trading, although Congress saw fit to pass bills that policed the board's activities. The Commodity Exchange Act of 1936, for example, regulated transactions on commodity futures exchanges.

As the twentieth century drew to a close, the legendary pit, so long the symbol of dizzying speculation, began to fade, as computers replaced the arcane practice of flashing hand signals to communicate over the racket of bellowing traders. In 2018, the *Wall Street Journal* quoted a trader, who said, "We're still buying and selling corn. We're still buying and selling bonds. But I'm doing it right now in front of six computer screens instead of 600 traders. It's not nearly as much fun." The pit, despite Norris's garish prose, was considered thrilling. Hence the necktie. There was even a joke: "Sure it's tough, but the hardest part is figuring out what to do with evenings and weekends."

5.

REGALIA WORN BY JOHN JONES AT THE FUNERAL OF ABRAHAM LINCOLN

Although Abraham Lincoln lived in and became a national figure in downstate Illinois, he had an ongoing relationship with Chicago. Lincoln was once even offered a law partnership there (he declined, preferring to remain where he was well-known). And although he did poorly in urban centers when he won the 1860 presidential election, he took Chicago by 2,500 votes—and it was the hometown of his rival, Stephen A. Douglas. Joseph Medill, the owner of the *Chicago Tribune* and a force in the establishment of the Republican Party, was Lincoln's friend and advisor, and he put his newspaper's clout at the service of his political campaigns. Medill had made the *Tribune* one of the nation's foremost antislavery journals, and in Lincoln, he believed he had found his man.

Chicagoans first heard of the lanky young downstate politico as early as 1839, when the *Chicago American* reported, "A. Lincoln and Cyrus Walker, Esq., candidates for Whig electors, have been addressing the people on subjects of national politics, etc." Lincoln appears to have first visited Chicago in 1847, when he attended the Rivers and Harbors Convention, an event held to pressure the federal government to fund river and harbor improvement. In his capacity as an attorney, Lincoln visited Chicago several times over the next dozen years, and in 1856, he campaigned in the city for John C. Frémont, the presidential candidate of the newly formed Republican Party. We even know that, in 1857, while representing the Illinois Central Railroad in a court case, Lincoln went to the theater to see a comedy called *Toodles*. It was in Chicago that Lincoln was nominated as the 1858 Republican

The sash worn by John Jones at the funeral of Abraham Lincoln. *Chicago History Museum, ICHi-066081.*

candidate for the U.S. Senate and challenged his Democratic opponent in a series of debates, which became the legendary Lincoln-Douglas debates. These debates were what made Lincoln a viable presidential prospect (none of the debates were held in Chicago, however). Finally, it was in Chicago that Republicans held the convention that nominated Lincoln for the presidency. It met in a new convention center on Lake and Market Streets (now Wacker Drive) called the Wigwam. Lincoln never saw Chicago again, but after his death on April 15, 1865, his body was placed on a funeral train that made a mournful three-week journey across America, stopping in the Windy City on May 1 and 2. The procession on May 1 lasted for four hours; the crowds that lined the streets were large but eerily quiet. The only sound was a forty-piece military band playing "The Lincoln Requiem." The houses and storefronts were festooned with black-and-white crepe. And among the twelve pallbearers listed in the *Tribune* was one "Hon. J.R. Jones," who had a story of his own.

Jones was born in North Carolina in 1816 to a German American father surnamed Bromfield and a biracial mother whose last name was Jones—this made him officially Black. In 1844, he married the daughter of an African American blacksmith in Alton, Illinois, and the couple moved to Chicago, where Jones opened a flourishing tailor shop. Jones became a notary public, and in 1871, he became a Cook County commissioner. Before the Civil War, Illinois had a series of "Black Laws" that curtailed many rights for African Americans. For example, African Americans couldn't make contracts or testify against a White person in court, and they had no right to an education. Jones was most proud of his ongoing efforts to repeal these laws, which didn't happen until 1865, only three months before Lincoln's death. Jones was also prominent in the abolitionist movement, which was strong in Chicago. A downstate newspaper even lambasted the city as a "sink hole of abolition." *Western Citizen*, one of the nation's leading abolitionist newspapers, was published in Chicago, and the city was home to the Chicago Anti-Slavery Society and one of the major stops on the Underground Railroad, which transported escaped slaves to the North. We do not know if Lincoln and Jones ever met, but it seems likely. Lincoln was the standard bearer of the abolitionist Republican Party, and the fact that Jones was selected to march in the funeral cortege wearing the shoulder regalia seen here suggests some sort of relationship. It consists of black crepe streamers edged with black-and-white silk ribbon attached to a rosette.

Reporting on the Lincoln funeral in Chicago, the *Tribune* said, "He comes back to us, his work finished, the Republic vindicated, his enemies overthrown and suing for peace; but alas! He returns with the crown of martyrdom." The reporter who wrote the account called Chicago "the city that he loved and that loved him." When John Jones died fourteen years later, that same newspaper praised him in a lengthy obituary: "He is an instance of a man who, belonging to a despised and proscribed race, and denied in youth the advantages of education, succeeded in working his way up to become prominent among his people, a respected member of the community, and the first one of his race who ever held an elective office in Cook County, and probably in Illinois."

6.

WATER TOWER PEWTER SOUVENIR

Even though the Irish playwright Oscar Wilde famously called it "a castellated monstrosity with pepper boxes stuck all over it," the 182-foot Water Tower is an emblem of Chicago—the kind of thing visitors take home as a souvenir, as this vintage memento demonstrates. Antique postcards of the Water Tower are readily available, and its image has appeared on plates, spoons, magnets, ashtrays, T-shirts, coasters and stick pins; it has even been turned into bracelet charms, Christmas ornaments and snow globes. It also inspired the look of the White Castle hamburger outlets. The tower's aura is largely due to the fact that it survived the Great Fire of 1871, which made the structure a symbol of the city's indomitable resilience. But the Water Tower was built for a practical reason—as part of an ongoing effort to provide the Windy City with pure water.

In Chicago's earliest days it had no sewers. Ditches ran down the sides of the streets, and the waste that poured into them was eventually washed into the Chicago River by the rain. This was not a long-term solution because the city was regularly struck by epidemics—most notably, cholera, which was traced to the filthy water. Sewers were installed in the mid-1850s, but they were built above ground and covered with soil, new streets and sidewalks, which meant the streets were then higher than the front doors of the buildings. A solution was found, but it was a drastic one. Over the course of the next two decades, buildings were raised up by hydraulic jacks. George M. Pullman, who went on to be famous for his railroad sleeping cars, was one of the busiest building boosters. The most impressive lifting was

Water tower pewter souvenir.
Author's collection.

that of the Briggs House, a five-story, twenty-two-thousand-ton hotel, which was jacked up five feet, all while the establishment functioned as usual, with patrons coming and going. The costs of raising the buildings were left to the property owners, some of whom avoided the expense by moving their front doors to the second level. This is why, in some Chicago neighborhoods, one can find old homes with second-story windows at sidewalk level. Other owners of older wooden buildings opted to put them on rollers and move them to distant neighborhoods.

The new sewers worked, but sewage still poured into the river and then into Lake Michigan, which became increasingly befouled. This was a problem, as the lake was the source of the city's drinking water. Engineers realized that the water would need to be drawn from the lake much further from shore, so a two-mile tunnel was built beneath its waters and connected to a water intake at the "Two Mile Crib." Beginning in 1866, the water pumped from the crib was piped to the Chicago Avenue Pumping Station, the building adjacent to the Water Tower. The tower itself contained a 135-foot iron standpipe that controlled the water pressure.

Yet, as the city continued to grow, so did the vile effluvium, ever further into Lake Michigan and past the Two Mile Crib. City hall then opted for one of Chicago's most celebrated feats: it was going to reverse the course of the Chicago River. Doing so would send the waste not into the lake, but down the Illinois and Michigan Canal, to the Desplaines River, then the Illinois River and, finally, the Mississippi River (too bad for the downstate population). By 1871, the canal had been deepened and pumping stations had been built, but, as luck would have it, it was inadequate during heavy rains. It would back up, and toxic sludge would once again gush into the lake. The City of Big Shoulders rolled up its sleeves, and at a price of $30 million (ten times the cost of the 1871 project), it dug the Sanitary and Ship Canal, which finally solved the problem. More land was excavated during this canal's construction than in the building of the Panama Canal, and the American Society of Civil Engineering called it one of the greatest engineering feats in U.S. history.

The architect of the Water Tower was William Warren (better known as "W.W.") Boyington (1818–1898), who, like many important figures in Chicago's early history, came from the Northeast (he was born in Massachusetts and trained in New York). He was an exceedingly busy architect in mid-nineteenth-century Chicago, and he once said (with some exaggeration, perhaps) that if all the buildings he had designed were laid end to end, they would stretch for thirty miles. When Boyington held a grand fête to celebrate his fiftieth wedding anniversary in 1889, the *Chicago Tribune* hailed him as "the father of Chicago architecture" and said, "Nearly every building of importance in the city is the child or grandchild of Mr. Boyington's brain." His profile is much lower today, not only because so many great architects came after him, but because so few of his major buildings have survived: the original Palmer House, the Sherman House, the first Board of Trade Building, the Royal Insurance Building, the Grand Pacific Hotel, the Rock Island Depot—all gone. But the Water Tower, probably the most beloved landmark in the Windy City, remains.

7.

MARSHALL FIELD'S CHRISTMAS BOX

There was a time when few things delighted a Chicagoan more than finding one of these red boxes beneath the Christmas tree. During the rest of the year, Marshall Field's signature color was green, but Christmas changed everything.

The mid-nineteenth century was the age of the "merchant princes" who founded great department stores, such as Edward Filene, John Wanamaker, Joseph Hudson, Adam Gimbel, Rowland Macy and, in London, Harry Selfridge, who learned the business working at Field's. In 1921, the *Chicago Tribune* ran an article called "How to See Chicago." It began with the "Great Stores" and called State Street "the largest shopping district on earth." Its list of department stories starts with Marshall Field & Co., and continues, heading south, with Charles A. Stevens & Bros.; Mandel Brothers; Carson, Pirie, and Scott; Hillman's; the Boston Store; the Fair; and Rothschild's—all on one street.

Department stores still exist. If a department store is defined as a place where you can buy merchandise ranging from tools to clothes to toys—and maybe have lunch—then Target is a department store. But shopping at Target today is worlds away from shopping at Field's in the 1890s, where an official greeter would welcome you and smiling salespeople would courteously help you select what you needed. A Target store is hardly a tourist attraction, but Field's was one of Chicago's don't-miss sights. It was common at railroad stations, and, later, airports, to see departing visitors toting multiple green shopping bags inscribed with "Marshall Field's" and the logo of its landmark clock.

Marshall Field's Christmas box. *Author's collection.*

Marshall Field (1834–1906) was born in Massachusetts, and at the age of twenty-one, he left for Chicago, which he saw as a land of opportunity. He found a job at a wholesale firm, worked hard, learned the business and, before long, was a partner in the firm of Farwell, Field and Company. The new company then added Levi Leiter as a junior partner, and Farwell left to go into real estate. At the time, the reigning merchant prince in Chicago was Potter Palmer, but he wanted to slow down, so he sold his entire retail business to Field and Leiter, who became owners of the finest dry goods store west of the Alleghenies. In 1868, Field and Leiter opened a store at the corner of State and Washington Streets, where Macy's is today. Three years later, it was destroyed in the Great Fire. The present twelve-story building was completed in four stages between 1902 and 1914 (the Annex on Wabash Avenue dates back to 1893).

Field bought out Leiter in 1880, and the business simply became Marshall Field & Co. One of the most often-told stories is about a time when Field found a salesclerk arguing with a female customer. The clerk explained, "I'm settling a complaint." Field shot back, "No you're not! Give the lady what she wants." Whether or not Field actually said that, thousands of customers trusted what became the store's slogan. The patrons were mostly women, as were the staff. Prices were fixed, with no unladylike haggling.

Marshall Field's department store. *Library of Congress.*

The store was luxurious but not snobbish; Field ordered his clerks to treat both the rich and poor with respect. As Gayle Soucek explained in *Marshall Field's: The Store that Helped Build Chicago*, "It was a store where a lady could purchase a ridiculously extravagant Persian cashmere shawl for $1,200 or a yard of calico for less than a dime and still receive unerringly superior service." Field's grew into the biggest retail store on earth. It had a dome of Tiffany glass, capacious restrooms, a bookstore, a parlor, a medical dispensary, a nursery, a multilingual information desk and meeting rooms for women's groups. The Walnut Room (1907) was the first full-service restaurant in a department store, and by 1920, Field's had seven places in which customers could dine.

Like other great urban department stores, by the end of the twentieth century, Field's had lost some of its magnetism. Suburban branches drained off downtown customers, while stores from elsewhere, such as Nordstrom's, Nieman-Marcus and Saks Fifth Avenue, opened competitive units in Chicago. And the rise of online shopping, of course, was a severe blow to retailers everywhere. Chicagoans were dismayed when Macy's acquired and renamed the Loop store in 2006.

In its prime, Field's was especially active on Christmas, which made it a magical world to children. The Walnut Room featured what Field's claimed to be the world's tallest indoor Christmas tree. The store's cavernous interior was festooned with garlands of evergreens, while giant candy canes and snowflakes hung from the ceilings and skylights. The most anticipated attractions were the widow displays. In 1944, window designer John Moss created a series of panels narrating the poem "A Visit from St. Nicholas," and two years later, Field's windows introduced the store's own creation—chubby Uncle Mistletoe, who flew around the world clad in a red coat and black top hat spreading Christmas cheer. Many of the store's red Christmas boxes seem to have survived. This is not only because they were treasured; it appears customers would reuse them, filling them with merchandise bought in lesser stores and presenting them as gifts from the incomparable Marshall Field & Co.

8.

CHICAGO FIRE WALKING STICK

I t might seem peculiar, even macabre, to collect souvenirs from a massive tragedy. We don't wear jewelry made from the wreckage of the World Trade Center. But Chicagoans thought differently about the Great Fire. As the *Chicago Tribune* explained, "Everyone wanted a relic of the greatest fire in the most marvelous city in the world." Youngsters set up shop on street corners, peddling mementos, such as the "fused" object—globs of melted marbles, bottles, pins, buttons and the like. For years, tourists could visit the "Original Relic House" and see tools, toys, bottles, sewing machines and other objects that had survived the blaze. Even the Relic House itself was built from melted stone and metals. The bell that came crashing down when the city hall/courthouse was destroyed was purchased by one Thomas B. Bryan, who resold it to a company that turned it into coins and miniature "charm bells," as well as the head of this walking stick, which belonged to Judge Joseph Mead Bailey, whose name is inscribed on the neck. (Bailey later became chief justice of the Illinois Supreme Court.)

The Great Chicago Fire, which began on October 8, 1871, and raged for thirty-six hours, torched an area four miles long and one mile wide, including the heart of the city; it consumed nearly 18,000 buildings and rendered some 100,000 people homeless. The New England poet John Greenleaf Whittier composed an elegy that concluded, "The City of the West Is Dead." But many neighborhoods remained intact. Three-quarters of the buildings in the city still stood, and the same percentage of Chicagoans still had homes. The Union Stock Yard was distant from the fire,

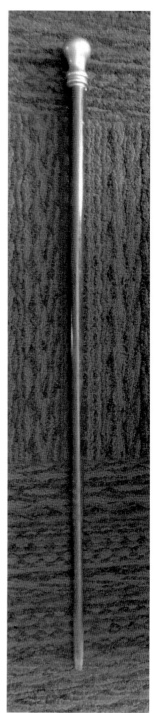

Chicago Fire walking stick. *Author's collection.*

and most railroad terminals and grain elevators survived, as did even most of the lumberyards. On October 11, the *Tribune* announced, "Cheer up…looking upon the ashes of thirty years' accumulations, the people of this once beautiful city have resolved that CHICAGO SHALL RISE AGAIN." Chicagoan William Bross hurriedly made a speaking tour of the East, announcing, "Go to Chicago now! Young men, hurry there! Old men, send your sons! Women, send your husbands! You will never again have such a chance to make money." Clearly, those who coveted relics viewed the blaze not as a calamity as much as an opportunity.

So, after the "Great Fire" came the "Great Rebuilding." The downtown area became a frenzy of construction; within months, it was estimated that workers were laying one million bricks per day. The rebuilding, however, was not without its disputes—ones that still resonate with Chicagoans. First came the

Chicago after the Great Fire. *Library of Congress.*

matter of how to help the homeless. Many citizens needed aid, but the degree of charity was controversial. The argument among many was that able-bodied people should help themselves, that there was a difference between the "worthy" and "unworthy" poor and that liberal charity could "corrupt" the lower classes. Second, the city's elite considered it obvious that all new construction should be done in brick and stone and that the city should order this through building codes, but people of moderate means saw this as an oppressive elitist mandate that would deny them affordable wooden homes. A compromise was reached when a bill was passed extending fire codes to a larger section of the city but leaving nearly the entire North Side—home to many of Chicago's immigrants—open to wooden construction. Finally, job seekers flooded into the city from all over the country, leading to an oversupply of workers and a drop in wages that alarmed the labor unions, especially those of the carpenters and bricklayers. The unions, however, were unable to muster the support they needed to call a strike.

There has been much speculation as to what Chicago would have been like had the fire never happened, and it's possible that some areas, having preserved older housing stock, would feel more like Boston or New York's Greenwich Village. The dumping of tons of debris into the lake formed a huge landfill that enabled the city to build Grant Park, which might not have been there otherwise. Most important, historians say the Great Rebuilding attracted talented architects from across the nation. Of the famous architects associated with the early years of what is known as the Chicago School of Architecture (Daniel Burnham, Louis Sullivan, Dankmar Adler, William Le Baron Jenney, John Wellborn Root, Charles Bowler Atwood, Frank Lloyd Wright, William Holabird and Martin Roche), none were born in the city—although, Roche grew up there—and it's doubtful that the few who were in Chicago before 1871 would have had the opportunities presented by the Great Rebuilding. In 1871, there was about 300,000 square feet of office space in the Loop. Twenty years later, there was about two million square feet, as Chicagoans had invented the skyscraper.

9.

BRONZE ROSETTE FROM THE HOME LIFE INSURANCE BUILDING

When the year 2000 was approaching, a book appeared that ranked the most important people who lived in the previous millennium (*1,000 Years, 1,000 People: Ranking the Men and Women Who Shaped the Millennium* by Agnes Hooper Gottlieb, Henry Gottlieb, Barbara Bowers and Brent Bowers). A Chicagoan named William Le Baron Jenney came in at number eighty-nine. That was higher than Marconi, Goethe, Van Gogh, Eli Whitney, Susan B. Anthony, Frank Lloyd Wright, Jane Austen and James Madison, to mention just a few. This might be cause for many Chicagoans to ask, "William Le Baron Jenney *who?*"

The answer to this is that Jenney was regarded as the founder of the Chicago School of Architecture, the most famous school of architecture in American history. He was also known as the father of the skyscraper, one of the most impactful inventions to ever come out of Chicago.

Jenney was born in Fairhaven, Massachusetts, in 1832. He took part in the California gold rush, stayed a while in the Philippines, and then entered school at Harvard. At the age of twenty-one, he went to Paris to study engineering (one of his roommates was the painter James McNeill Whistler, and tower designer Gustave Eiffel was in his class). During the Civil War, Jenney served as an engineer for both Ulysses S. Grant and William Tecumseh Sherman. He built fortifications, razed rebel bridges and learned a lot about iron construction. After the war, he settled in Chicago and was there when the Great Fire destroyed most of the city. It was a tragedy, but it was also quite an opportunity for architects.

Left: Bronze rosette from the Home Life Insurance Building. *Chicago History Museum, ICHi-066335.*

Opposite: Home Life Insurance Building. *Library of Congress.*

Jenney was sometimes considered more of an engineer than an architect. His building designs were not especially exciting, but the structural principles behind them were revolutionary. His innovations led to what is known as metal-frame, curtain-wall or skeletal construction. The method involves the erection of a metal cage on which the walls of the building are hung like curtains (or like skin on a skeleton). Because the walls don't bear the building's weight, they can be thin and light and contain a great number of large windows, which were prized for bringing in light and air.

The object seen here is a bronze rosette from Jenney's Home Life Insurance Building (1885). It was salvaged from the rubble when the building was demolished in 1931. Many histories of architecture state that this building was the first skyscraper. Whether that's true depends on how "skyscraper" is defined. If one requirement is that the building is 100 percent metal-frame construction, the Home Life Insurance Building wouldn't qualify because it used granite in its base and brick for the party walls. But it was almost a technical quibble. The fact remains that the edifice was a breakthrough in every sense of the word, especially in its use of a steel framework for the upper floors, which was the first time steel was used in skyscraper construction— and steel henceforth became universal in tall buildings. In any case, the first skyscraper to be entirely raised on a skeletal structure appears to have been Chicago's Manhattan Building, which also happened to be the work of William Le Baron Jenney. Fortunately, that building still stands.

As important as Jenney's architectural and engineering originality was, his mentoring of the next generation of Chicago architects was just as

THE CHICAGO BUILDING OF THE HOME INSURANCE CO.

OF NEW YORK

essential. The architects who worked for Jenney included Daniel Burnham, Louis Sullivan, William Holabird, Martin Roche and Howard Van Doren Shaw—a who's who of the creators of what is now known as the Chicago School of Architecture.

The authors of *1,000 Years, 1,000 People* got it right.

10.

HAYMARKET AFFAIR LAPEL PIN

For most of its history, Chicago has played an outsized role in the American labor movement, and this macabre brass lapel pin is a memento of one of its most dramatic moments. It was worn as a gesture of protest after four men were hanged for their connections to the incident known as either the Haymarket Riot or the Haymarket Affair, depending on one's political views.

A labor movement began forming in Chicago as early as the 1850s and was energized during the Civil War, when unions began demanding an eight-hour workday. The first major labor turbulence in American history was the great Railroad Strike of 1877. Although it began in West Virginia, it spread to other locales, including Chicago, where the military joined local militia and police to put down mob violence. At least fifty civilians were killed, and in the aftermath, Chicago became recognized as the center of American radicalism.

The events that led to the Haymarket Affair began on May 1, 1886 (the first "May Day"), when some forty thousand Chicago workers went on strike. Two days later, picketers battled police and detectives at the McCormick Reaper Works. Two men were killed and many more were wounded. German-born labor leader and newspaper editor August Spies hastily wrote a leaflet that called for workmen to arm themselves, while the *Chicago Tribune* threatened, "Every lamp post in Chicago will be decorated with a Communistic carcass if necessary"—remarks that reveal the fear of revolution that gripped the propertied classes at the time. Labor leaders arranged a demonstration in

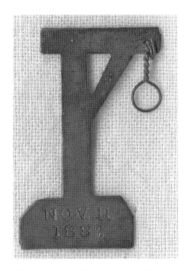

Haymarket Affair lapel pin. *Chicago History Museum, ICHi-066273.*

Haymarket Square on the West Side on the evening of May 4. Rain held the numbers to a disappointing three thousand, which had dwindled to about three hundred when Samuel Fielden, the last speaker, mounted the platform. All seemed peaceful enough. Mayor Carter Harrison stopped by and saw nothing alarming. But something Fielden said frightened a couple of detectives, who asked the local police to intervene. Just as police were shutting things down, a bomb was tossed from an alley and exploded. At the same time, the police opened fire, scattering the panicked crowd (to this day, no one is sure whether the bombing or the shooting happened first). Seven policemen were killed, as were an unknown number of civilians.

The bomb thrower's identity remains unknown, but all indications point to Rudolph Schnaubelt, who was briefly detained and then fled the city. Eight suspected radicals were arrested, charged and put on trial. Spies Albert Parsons, Adolph Fischer and George Engel were found guilty and hanged on November 11, 1887, the date commemorated on this pin. Louis Lingg committed suicide before he could be executed. Fielden and Michael Schwab were sentenced to life in prison, and Oscar Neebe received a fifteen-year sentence. In 1893, Illinois governor John Peter Altgeld, convinced that the trial had been characterized by "hysteria, packed juries, and a biased judge," issued pardons for Fielden, Schwab and Neebe. When warned that this was an act of political suicide, Altgeld said, "No man has the right to allow his ambition to stand in the way of the performance of a simple act of justice."

Chicago's next great labor upheaval was the Pullman Strike of 1894, which is discussed in the chapter titled "Pullman Porter Cap." Things again reached a boiling point during World War I. Between 1914 and 1920, more than three thousand strikes occurred in the United States every year. Because the products of the steel mills and packinghouses were in great demand, as were the workers because of a labor shortage, the 300,000-member Chicago Federation of Labor (CFL) saw its chance to demand pay raises and an eight-hour workday. In 1919, Chicago steelworkers staged a massive walkout (see "Steel Mill Postage Stamp"). Chicago was also home to the Industrial

A contemporary depiction of the Haymarket Affair. *Library of Congress.*

Workers of the World (IWW), nicknamed "the Wobblies." This was a radical organization founded in 1905, and it advocated for the abolition of the employer class and terrified the plutocrats. In September 1917, federal agents raided the IWW headquarters. The following year, 97 Wobblies were put on trial in Chicago; 95 were convicted and given sentences ranging from ten days to twenty years. Labor unions finally achieved legal recognition in the 1930s, although strikes still occurred. However, with the steady deindustrialization of the city in the late twentieth century, when a strike happened, it was more likely to involve schoolteachers than industrial workers.

It took decades for American-organized labor to recover its reputation after the Haymarket Affair, and the fact that five of the accused instigators were German-born only intensified an already pervasive fear of immigrants. European-style anarchism and communism never seriously took hold in the United States, and the eight-hour workday did not become federal law until 1937. Americans at least got a new holiday out of it. May Day, first observed in Chicago in 1886, is celebrated around the world, but not in the United States, where it still has communist connotations. In 1894, President Grover Cleveland signed the law creating Labor Day. It's observed not in May, but in September, when it's thought of mostly as the end of summer and the beginning of the school year.

11.

SILVER BOWL MADE BY FRANCES GLESSNER

his silver bowl was made by the heiress to one of Chicago's great fortunes. She did not let her pampered background limit her horizons. Frances Glessner (1878–1962) grew up at 1800 Prairie Avenue, an eighteen-thousand-square-foot castle in the center of a frighteningly rich neighborhood that contained more than ninety mansions, several of which were designed by the likes of Daniel Burnham, Richard Morris Hunt and H.H. Richardson—the most prestigious architects of the Gilded Age. The core of Chicago's first "Gold Coast," the neighborhood ran from Sixteenth Street to Twenty-Second Street (now Cermak Road), and contemporary guidebooks considered it a must-see. According to William H. Tyre, the author of *Chicago's Historic Prairie Avenue*, the thoroughfare "achieved a prominence in the late nineteenth century that will probably never again be achieved in Chicago." The first mansions were built in the 1850s, but Prairie Avenue became chic when Chicago's tycoons moved in after the Great Fire of 1871. Among them were meatpacking giant Philip Armour, department store magnate Marshall Field and George M. Pullman of sleeping car fame. When activists wanted to protest the inequality of the era, they knew where to go. On Thanksgiving Day in 1884, a "poor people's march" was held on Prairie Avenue, the protestors insolently ringing the doorbells as they advanced.

Frances Glessner's father was John Jacob Glessner, a vice-president of the International Harvester Company. Like her brother, George, Frances was schooled at home and received an excellent education. She studied

A silver bowl made by Frances Glessner. *Glessner House.*

literature, the violin, dance, mathematics, science and art, and she learned to speak German, French and Italian. She also became skilled in sewing, china painting, jewelry making and silversmithing, as this elegant bowl shows. She also developed an early interest in medicine, and as a teen, she would accompany local doctors on their rounds. When she married Blewett Lee, a Northwestern law professor descended from the Lee family of Virginia, the music for the ceremony, which was held in the family home, was provided by members of the Chicago Symphony Orchestra (see "Theodore Thomas Memorial Arrangement").

The marriage didn't work out, and the couple divorced in 1914. Afterward, Frances Glessner Lee launched her surprising career as a founder of modern forensic science. When recovering in a hospital in 1929, she unexpectedly encountered a fellow patient who had been her brother's best friend at Harvard. He was Dr. George Burgess Magrath, an instructor in legal medicine at Harvard Medical School and the country's top expert in the application of medical knowledge to police work, especially crime scene investigation. Frances was fascinated. Under Magrath's guidance, she participated in autopsies and learned how to analyze a murder scene. She funded a Department of Legal Medicine at Harvard and donated a library of one thousand books. As recounted in *18 Tiny Deaths: The Untold Story of Frances Glessner Lee and the Invention of Modern Forensics* by Bruce

Goldfarb, Frances's most innovative contribution to forensic science was the construction of nineteen dollhouse-like rooms or dioramas (one was accidentally destroyed, leaving eighteen). They contain miniature detailed death scenes (murder, suicide, accidents and natural deaths) based on real events, and she called them "The Nutshell Studies of Unexplained Death," after the police maxim, "Convict the guilty, clear the innocent, and find the truth in a nutshell." Lee used the rooms in her crime seminars, in which students were required to study the models for ninety minutes and then present oral reports. Today, they are housed at the Maryland Medical-Legal Foundation and are still being used for training.

By the 1880s, the Prairie Avenue area was becoming begrimed by soot from the railroad, and Chicago's expanding vice district was growing uncomfortably near. In 1882, Potter Palmer, the owner of the Palmer House Hotel, began constructing a forty-two-room palace on North Lake Shore Drive. Gradually, Chicago's other millionaires followed his lead and relocated to what is today's Gold Coast. One by one, nearly all of the grand Prairie Avenue residences were demolished to make way for factories and other commercial enterprises. The last old-time resident was Addie Hibbard Gregory, who moved out in 1944, after living on the avenue for seventy-seven years. Her house was demolished soon after, but a few endured. When the Glessner House (1886) was threatened with demolition in the 1960s, Chicago's architectural and preservationist community rallied to save it, and today, it's at the center of the Prairie Avenue Historic District, which was designated in 1978. Other survivors include the Keith House (1870), which is believed to be the oldest on the street; the forty-three-room Marshall Field Jr. House (1884); the Coleman-Ames House (1886), which has been the site of several movie shoots; the Chateauesque Kimball House (1892); and the Reid House (1894), the first Chicago residence built with a steel frame and the only house on Prairie Avenue that has never been anything but a private home. The spaces between the surviving châteaux have been filled with luxury condominiums and stylish townhouses. Pullman and Field liked the neighborhood because they could walk to their downtown offices, which they regularly did, often together. Today, Prairie Avenue residents can do the same, which once again makes the street, after all these decades, an expensive place to live.

12.

STULL BICYCLE BUTTON

When surveying the history of Chicago, the word *capital* comes up a lot—as in "the railroad capital of America," "the meatpacking capital," "the capital of organized labor," "the jazz capital," "the world capital of the blues," " the postcard capital," "the candy capital of the world" and (if for just a few years) "the movie capital of the United States." Chicago was also, during the bicycle craze of the late nineteenth century, the bicycle capital. In 1896, it was reported that eighty-eight bicycle manufacturers were located in the Windy City, and two-thirds of all the bicycles produced in the United States were being built within 150 miles of Chicago. One of those manufacturers was the Curtis Machine Works, the makers of Stull bicycles.

This button is especially interesting because of its image of a woman riding a bicycle. At the time, the bicycle was considered one of the greatest forces in America for women's liberation. Susan B. Anthony, the leading suffragist, said that the bicycle "has done more to emancipate women than anything else in the world." After the introduction of two-wheel "safety bicycles" with pneumatic tires, women could ride out into the world without escorts or chaperones, which was immensely liberating. Also, because a woman could hardly ride a bicycle wearing an old-style corset or bustle, an upsurge of dress reform ensued. Out went the restrictive garments, and in came bloomers, which were named after Amelia Bloomer of Seneca Falls, New York. As early as 1851, Bloomer promoted a "freedom dress"—trousers clutched at the ankles beneath a dress that came just below the knees. A few women tried them, but they didn't really catch on until the bicycle boom. In 1895, the *New York Times* observed, "If it is true that without wheelwomen, there would be no dress reform, it is no less true that without dress reform, there would be no wheelwomen." In that same year, a reporter from the *Chicago Tribune* visited some city parks and found:

> *There were hundreds of bicycles out and, among them, more than the usual proportion of women, young and old, and where there was one woman attired in skirts, there were a dozen who wore bloomers of one sort or another. Some wore knickerbockers, some Turkish garments of such generous volume as to almost look like skirts, and others wore the zouave style of bifurcated clothing.*

Another garment was the "rainy day skirt," which could be surprisingly short—sometimes with an eight-inch hemline. It's difficult to tell, but it might be what the woman on this button is wearing. Leading the dress reform movement was Frances E. Willard of Evanston, Illinois, whom many then considered "the greatest American woman." In 1893, she presided over the opening of the Woman's Temple, an extraordinary Chicago skyscraper that was the headquarters of the organization she headed, the Women's Christian Temperance Union, and served as a rental property to fund the group's many progressive efforts. In 1895, Willard published *A Wheel within a Wheel*, a best-seller that relates how she learned to ride a bicycle at the age of fifty-three.

One reason Chicago became the bicycle capital was it was such a prodigious manufacturing center. Also, the city, being basically flat, was easy on riders, who valued its extensive park and boulevard system. Then, too, Chicago's bicycle organizations got pro-bicycle measures enacted, such as the paving of city streets. Finally, the city's medical establishment approved bicycling as a way to lure young men out of saloons and into the fresh air. The Chicago Cycling Club, founded in 1879, was the oldest and largest bicycling club in America, and it was just one of dozens of bicycling clubs in the city. In 1895, the Chicago Cycling Club opened an elegant new headquarters on Michigan Avenue that boasted a ballroom, a dining hall, reading

Stull bicycle button. *Author's collection.*

rooms, billiard parlors, showers, a "rubbing down" room and a chic women's auxiliary on the second floor. It was in that same year that Schwinn, one of America's most historic bicycle makers, opened its factory on the corner of Lake and Peoria Streets.

The arrival of the automobile spelled the end of the bicycle craze. But bicycling didn't die in Chicago—it just went into hibernation. In the 1970s, the city began developing a network of bicycle lanes and paths. A thirty-four-mile bicycle route opened in May 1971, and rush-hour bicycle lanes appeared a year later. In the 1990s, Mayor Richard M. Daley oversaw the construction of one hundred miles of on-street bike lanes and fifty miles of off-street trails, as well as the placement of bike racks on city buses and the installation of ten thousand sidewalk bike racks. In recent years, various organizations have been ranking U.S. cities for their bicycle friendliness, and Chicago invariably ranks in the top ten and is sometimes number one. In 2018, the city spent $53.5 million on bicycle-related infrastructure, a figure *Bicycling* magazine called "amazing." The magazine also praised Chicago's Divvy bike-sharing program and its success in separating pedestrians and bicycles on the lakefront bike path, which, given the Windy City's bicycling history, is not surprisingly the most heavily used bike trail in the nation.

13.

CHICAGO HOT DOG

The Chicago hot dog, is an image of the city just as much as the Wrigley Building or the "Bean." It's a beef hot dog with seven must-have ingredients (yellow mustard, chopped onions, a pickle spear, tomato slices, bright green pickle relish, sport peppers and celery salt) served on a poppy seed bun. Although today it's world-famous, getting to this exalted state was a long process that unfolded in three stages. First came the hot dog itself. Second came the piling on of the garnishes. Third came national recognition.

A "hot dog" is a frankfurter or a wiener. Today, the names are pretty much interchangeable, but frankfurters came from Frankfurt, Germany, and wieners came from Vienna (*Vienna* in German is *Wien*, pronounced "veen"). As for the Chicago hot dog itself, German immigrants brought franks and wieners to the city in the 1850s. David Berg & Co. has been turning out hot dogs in Chicago since 1860, and the hot dog behemoth Oscar Mayer got its start in the Windy City in 1883. (Although their product is no longer a true Chicago dog because they moved to Wisconsin in 1919.) Today, however, the odds are overwhelming that anyone patronizing one of the city's estimated 2,500 hot dog emporia will find the dogs to be from Vienna Beef, the company that dominates the market. Vienna Beef was the creation of Samuel Ladany and Emil Reichl, two young immigrants who were born in Hungary, trained as sausage makers in Vienna and came to Chicago in 1890. When the Columbian Exposition ("White City") opened in 1893, the pair saw their opportunity and set up a sausage cart. They

Chicago hot dog. *Photograph by author.*

did not sell within the fairgrounds but next to one of the entrances to the Midway section. They did so well that they were able open a store at 417 South Halsted Street. They didn't just serve walk-in customers but also supplied grocery stores and restaurants. Because the partners were Jewish, their sausages contained no pork, only beef—hence the name "Vienna Beef." In 1908, Vienna Beef organized a fleet of horse-drawn delivery wagons that, two decades later, were replaced with motorized vehicles. Samuel Ladany's sons, Jules and William, eventually took over the business and oversaw the opening of a large modern factory and the introduction of Vienna Beef products into supermarkets.

Next came the additions that made the Chicago hot dog so different from those of other cities. The source of this phenomenon is not as unambiguous as Vienna Beef, but hot dog historians cite the claims of one Abe Drexler, who, around 1932, opened an outlet called Fluky's on the corner of Halsted and Maxwell Streets in what was then a Jewish neighborhood. On July 29, 1976, a reporter from the *Chicago Tribune* interviewed Drexler, who said that, at first, his father ran a fruit stand, but then "the fruit stand was converted into a hot dog stand." He continued, "I was 19 when I started working there.…We sold hot dogs for a nickel apiece, seven items for a nickel: the hot dog, onions, pickle, piccalilli, French fries, lettuce, hot peppers." Drexler's list of condiments is not identical to those used today, but it's close. During hard times, the abundance of ingredients available for a nickel was a bargain, and the sausages became known as "Depression dogs." In his 2009 book, *Hot Dog*, Chicago historian Bruce Kraig recounts talking to people who remembered the Depression dog and concluded that other vendors, in addition to Fluky's, were adding toppings to their hot dogs. Kraig theorized that, while Germans brought mustard, pickles and celery salt, Greeks and Italians contributed relish, tomatoes and sport peppers (think *giardiniera*). The concoction became known as "dragged through the garden." In the 1970s, Chicagoans began to realize the local hot dog was something special. They began comparing the best vendors and insisted on the formulaic ingredients and a strict ban on ketchup. On June 6, 1971, the *Tribune* ran a story called "The Great Chicago Hot Dog Quest," in which the reporter rated various dogs around the city. In the 1983 book *Hot Dog Chicago: A Native's Dining Guide* by Rich Bowen and Dick Fay, the authors sampled hot dog outlets and listed as orthodox the seven now-standard toppings.

Finally, the Chicago hot dog went national. In 1985, the *Philadelphia Inquirer* ran a long story about a new joint on South Street in Philadelphia called Franks-A-Million that was selling Chicago-style Vienna Beef hot dogs. The article explained, "A Chicago red hot is a kosher-style, all-beef hot dog that—heaven forbid!—is never considered junk food or a fast-food snack. To a Chicagoan, it's dinner or lunch—possibly even breakfast." A year later, Chicago hot dogs were reportedly available in Toronto, and a year after that, they were available in Quincy, Massachusetts, and Fort Lauderdale, where they were served with "Flamingo fries." In his 2008 book, *Never Put Ketchup on a Hot Dog*, Vienna Beef executive Bob Schwartz listed Chicago hot dog vendors in Tampa; Anchorage; Minneapolis; Honolulu; Milwaukee; St. Louis; Boulder, Colorado; Burbank, California; and other locations. Today, the glorified encased meat object has become one of America's most recognized regional food specialties, along with New York bagels, New Orleans po'boys, Maryland crab cakes, Pennsylvania scrapple, Maine lobster rolls and other esteemed edibles meriting a traveler's detour and a citation in any serious guidebook.

14.

POSTCARD FERRIS WHEEL

The world's first Ferris wheel, the highlight of Chicago's 1893 "White City" Columbian Exposition, was a tremendous hit. This can be seen from the many souvenirs and tributes it inspired. There were, for example, pop songs, such as "The Song of the Ferris Wheel," "The Ferris Wheel Waltz and Polka" and "The Ferris Wheel March and Two-Step." There were Ferris wheel glass paperweights, sterling silver spoons, stereoscope cards and so many medals an entire book has been devoted to them (*Ferris Wheel Medals of the 1893 World's Columbian Exposition* by Steven A. Middleton). But the most unusual item was this Ferris wheel postcard rack, which was made by the Alfred Holzman Co. of Chicago, a major manufacturer of postcards. It's nearly four feet high, holds five thousand cards and was sold for fifteen dollars. For the Columbian Exposition, several publishers, most notably Charles W. Goldsmith, issued America's first picture postcards, which started the American postcard industry. This postcard wheel is another forgotten example of how Chicago once made such a huge variety of consumer products. The Windy City was once the world's leading producer of postcards (the postcard capital). Even larger than Holzman was the Curt Teich Company, whose archives, now housed in Chicago's Newberry Library, contain over 360,000 images.

Seeing a photograph of the White City's astonishing Court of Honor makes one understand how it inspired Chicagoan L. Frank Baum's Emerald City in *The Wonderful Wizard of Oz* (1900) and Walt Disney's Disneyland. (Disney's father, Elias, was a carpenter who helped build the fair.) The Paris

Postcard Ferris wheel. *Courtesy of the Newberry.*

Left: The Ferris wheel at the Columbian Exposition. *Library of Congress*.

Below: The Court of Honor at Chicago's "White City." *Library of Congress*.

Exposition of 1889 covered 160 acres, while the Columbian Exposition covered 633. Nearly all the primary buildings were designed in a neoclassical style, meant to evoke imperial Rome. Bright white, they gleamed in the summer sun and were even more glittering at night, when they were lit up by thousands of electric light bulbs. It's estimated one out of every four Americans visited the fair; on October 9, 1893 ("Chicago Day"), a record 716,881 visitors flooded into the exposition.

The primary purpose of the fair was to celebrate the four-hundredth anniversary of Christopher Columbus's arrival in the New World, but the exhibits constituted an encyclopedia of American innovation and expertise. Technological wonders abounded—agricultural machines; steam locomotives; gas engines; refrigerators; aluminum alloys; Edison's kinetoscope; examples of steelmaking and bridge engineering; and, especially, anything to do with electricity, which was acclaimed as the force of the future. The emphasis on technology was apparent in the names of the massive buildings that surrounded the Court of Honor: Manufactures and Liberal Arts, Electricity, Mines, Transportation, Machinery and Agriculture. The fair also featured pavilions from nineteen countries and thirty-eight states, each displaying their particular achievements. The most acclaimed building, however, was the Palace of Fine Arts, which is the Museum of Science and Industry today. It's the exposition's only surviving building in Chicago.

The Ferris wheel was the result of a competition to create an attraction to outdo the Eiffel Tower of the Paris Exposition. Many ideas came in, and some were really loopy (for example: a passenger-filled car that would be pushed off a tower and then snapped back by a rubber cable), but the winner came from an engineer from Pittsburgh named George Washington Ferris Jr. The wheel was 264 feet tall, and each car was the size of a bus. It stood in a separate area called the Midway, where people could have fun, see shows, dine and gape at the wonders of exotic cultures. Here, there was the Ostrich Farm, the Bedouin Encampment, the Dahomey Village, the Bulgarian Curiosity Shop, the Brazilian Music Hall, Sitting Bull's Camp, the Vienna Café, the Japanese Tea House, the Irish Village, the Hungarian National Orpheum, the French Cider Press, the Lapland Village (complete with reindeer) and the popular Street in Cairo, where viewers could see the spicy "hootchy-cootchy" dance. Besides the Ferris wheel, the adventurous could ride the Ice Railway, a kind of rollercoaster with a route that was chilled by frozen ammonia gas, and the Captive Balloon, which would carry between fifteen and twenty passengers 1,493 feet up while secured by cables (sadly, a thunderstorm wrecked it before the fair was over).

Although the fair was meant to display the wonders of American creativity, Chicago's city leaders also intended it to demonstrate that Chicago had arrived as one of the great cities of the world—and it worked. The 27.5 million people who came to the fair were impressed, but for many, the biggest surprise was not the fair itself but the city that hosted it. In 1893, François Edmond Bruwaert, a French diplomat, wrote an essay for a French journal in which he described what his readers would find if they went to the fair:

> *It will not be…the exposition itself that will most surprise the foreigner who is enterprising enough to come as far as Chicago. The most beautiful exhibition will be Chicago itself, its citizens, its business, its institutions, its progress. Those who come here will wonder how, in less than fifty years, that is, in less than a man's lifetime, it has been possible to transform a swamp, producing only a sort of wild onion, into a powerful and flourishing city.*

15.

CRACKER JACK COMMEMORATIVE CANISTER

Although no convincing evidence exists of Cracker Jack being introduced at Chicago's Columbian Exposition of 1893—as is often claimed—nothing kept the makers of the popular confection from producing a centennial commemorative canister in 1993 that showed the great Ferris wheel and other features of the "White City." It's a long-told story that's too good to discard.

Chicago was once known as "the candy capital of the world." For much of the twentieth century, Chicago made about one-third of all the candy in the United States; more than one hundred factories were employing some twenty-five thousand workers. As early as 1884, the National Confectioners Association, representing sixty-nine companies, was born in Chicago. As recounted by author Leslie Goddard in *Chicago's Sweet Candy History*, the city's candy industry owed much of its success to European candymakers, especially those from Germany and Italy, who brought skills they had acquired in their homelands. Also, as with other Windy City industries, the railroad network and the Great Lakes shipping lanes facilitated importing raw materials, like milk and corn sugar, and transporting finished products. Finally, long winters extended the candymaking season in the days before air conditioning.

One of the first Chicago candy firms was Bunte Brothers, established in 1876 by two brothers from Germany and a friend. They were famous for their caramels and went on to create Diana "Stuft," the first candies with a hard shell and a soft center, and Tangos, a peanut-maple-marshmallow

Cracker Jack commemorative canister. *Author's collection.*

confection. Although they didn't invent candy canes, they patented a candy cane manufacturing machine that made these hangable treats a Christmas staple. Other Chicago candy operations have included Reed Candy Co. (1883), the makers of Butter Scotch Patties; Ferrara Candy Co. (1908), the makers of Jordan almonds, Lemonheads and Jujyfruits; Peerless Confection Co. (1914), the makers of Peermints; American Licorice Co. (1914), the makers of Snaps; Williamson Candy Co. (1920), the makers of Oh! Henry; Fanny May (1920); DeMet's (1923), the makers of Turtles; Flavour Candy Co. (1925), the makers of Chicken Bones; and Blommer Chocolate (1939). The Curtiss Candy Co. (1916), the makers of Baby Ruth and Butterfinger, seems to have been the first to package candies specifically for Halloween trick-or-treating. In 1922, E.J. Brach, founded in 1904, built the largest candy factory in the United States on Chicago's West Side; by the 1940s, it covered over two million square feet and employed 2,500 workers. Mars Inc., the makers of Snickers, Milky Way and M&Ms, was founded in 1911 in Tacoma, Washington, but relocated to Chicago in 1929. Similarly, Tootsie Rolls were invented in New York, but Tootsie Rolls Industries moved its production to Chicago in 1968. And then, of course, there was the empire founded by chewing gum magnate William Wrigley, who came to Chicago from Pennsylvania in 1891 and, two years later, began selling Spearmint and Juicy Fruit. Chicago candy makers invested heavily in advertising, and Wrigley led them all. It's hard to imagine Chicago without the Wrigley Building and Wrigley Field.

As for Cracker Jack, it began with Frederick William Rueckheim, who came to the United States from Germany in 1869. He saw opportunity in the rebuilding of Chicago after the Great Fire and moved to the city in 1871. He first sold popcorn from a wagon and was so successful that he brought over his younger brother, Louis, and formed F.W. Rueckheim & Bro. Somewhere along the way, they got the idea of caramelizing popcorn. They might have sold it at the Columbian Exposition, but there is no record of it. There is, however, an article from the March 8, 1896 edition of the *Chicago Tribune* with the title "Do Not Taste It. If You Do You, Will Part with Your Money Easy." The author reported that Cracker Jack was invented "only a short time ago" and exclaimed, "'Tis enough to say that the more Cracker Jack you eat, the more you'll want. Those who taste it actually crave it." But the report reassures readers: "It is perfectly harmless, not only harmless but healthful." Key to the product's success was the invention of a moisture-proof wax paper package and, of course, putting a prize in every box, which started in 1912.

In the twenty-first century, the Chicago candy industry began to melt like a chocolate bar in the sun. It didn't disappear, but several factors drove its decline. Weight-conscious Americans began to worry about sugar in their diets, and, although sugar consumption actually rose nationwide, eschewing candy made consumers feel they were at least trying, and the consumption of sweet snacks dropped. Candymakers complained about high labor costs and burdensome government regulations and pointed to the high cost of sugar, which they blamed on the federal government's policy of protecting domestic sugar by restricting imports. As for Chicago, many local brands were bought by the conglomerates Mars and Hershey. One segment of the candy business, however, flourished in Chicago—high-end gourmet chocolate. Prestige chocolate outlets included Vosges, Veruca, Katherine Anne, Teuscher, Leonidas and Royce. In 2017, *Crain's Chicago Business* ran a story titled "Downtown Becoming One Big Candy Shop" and profiled such posh emporiums as Kilwin's and L.A. Burdick, where a candy bar could cost thirteen dollars. At those prices, Chicago no longer needed two-million-square-foot candy factories.

16.

LOUIS SULLIVAN STOCK EXCHANGE KICK PLATE

Chicago architect Louis Sullivan (1856–1924) has long been a hero of modern architecture. A major reason for this was his famous saying, "form ever follows function" ("ever" is usually omitted), which modernists interpreted as a plea for unadorned utilitarian austerity. But if Sullivan was an apostle of plain directness, how does one explain this kick plate? A kick plate is an addition to the bottom of a door that protects it from damage, one of the humblest things a building can contain. That Sullivan chose to apply such a beautiful and fanciful design to a kick plate indicates there wasn't much of anything he didn't consider worth decorating. Ornamentation was not just of interest to him, it was crucial. In his book *Louis Henry Sullivan*, Mario Manieri Elia wrote that the original meaning of "form follows function" "struck far deeper and far more complex values than the cold, reductive interpretation conferred upon it by the modern movement."

Louis Sullivan was born in Boston, went to MIT and moved to Chicago, where his parents had been living for four years, in 1873. He left for a two-year stay at the Ecole des Beaux-Arts in Paris before returning to the Windy City, where the building boom after the Great Fire had put architects in great demand. After working in the studio of William Le Baron Jenney (see the "Bronze Rosette from the Home Life Insurance Building"), Sullivan formed a partnership with Dankmar Adler. They made an ideal team—Adler was a superb engineer, and Sullivan had a flair for design. Their Auditorium Theater (1889), the most expensive building to ever be erected in Chicago at

Louis Sullivan Stock Exchange kick plate. *Art Institute of Chicago.*

that time, made them famous. They followed it with the Wainwright Building in St. Louis, which was considered a giant step in skyscraper development, and the Schiller Theater Building in Chicago, a multi-use structure with a spectacular auditorium.

In 1893, Sullivan designed the Transportation Building for the Columbian Exposition. The multicolored structure, with its "Golden Door," clashed with the dominant neoclassical aspect of the "White City." Sullivan described the building as "elementary masses carrying elaborate decoration," which is not a bad description for many of his works. Sullivan earned further praise from modernists when he said, "The damage wrought by the World's Fair will last for half a century from its date, if not longer"—although he didn't make that complaint until 1924. The Transportation Building epitomized Sullivan's philosophy as it had expressed in his many writings, where he argued there was a need to devise a distinctively American style of architecture not beholden to the past as the Greco-Roman mockups of the 1893 fair were. Sullivan's originality arguably had less to do with his being a precursor of mid-twentieth century modernism (see "Mies van der

Rohe Apartments Playing Cards") and more with his encouragement of a distinctively American style.

The 1893 Chicago Stock Exchange, from which this kick plate was salvaged, was arguably Sullivan's masterpiece. The building employed steel-cage construction throughout, and Sullivan clad the exterior in beautifully ornamented terra-cotta. The building was demolished in 1972, but the entry arch was saved and placed outside the Art Institute, where it has since been called "the Wailing Wall of Chicago's preservation movement." The destruction of the Stock Exchange alerted Chicagoans to the precarious state of the city's great architecture, and the outrage sparked saved many historic buildings afterward.

Sullivan reached his peak in 1893 and then began to decline. Commissions dried up during and after the 1893 economic depression, although Sullivan and Adler managed to build the Guaranty Building in Buffalo (1896). Sullivan then broke with Adler, who was, unfortunately for Sullivan, the one with business savvy. Sullivan produced one more masterpiece, the Schlesinger & Meyer store of 1899 on State Street, which became the Carson, Pirie, Scott store in 1906 and the Sullivan Center in 2008. But the rest of his life was troubled by financial hardship, a scarcity of commissions and alcoholism. On April 13, 1924, the night before he died in a shabby Chicago hotel room, Sullivan was visited by his former employee Frank Lloyd Wright, who brought the man he called *Lieber Meister* (German for "Dear Master") a collection of drawings, most of which were Sullivan's. Wright once wrote, "Sullivan was essentially a lyric poet-philosopher interested in the sensuous experience of expressing inner rhythms evolving into a language of his own—ornament—in which to utter himself: unique among mankind."

The last building Sullivan designed was the Krause Music Store (1922), which still stands on North Lincoln Avenue. It's worth a visit to view its marvelous terra-cotta façade and its geometric and natural motifs—that is, for its ornamentation.

17

ALDERMAN MICHAEL "HINKY DINK" KENNA'S BADGE

I n the 1890s, Chicago was the scene of what were known as "the traction wars." An ambitious tycoon named Charles Tyson Yerkes wanted to acquire a monopoly of the city's highly profitable streetcar system (to which he had made significant improvements), and he needed the city council to grant him franchises to operate on public streets and to extend his transit leases for fifty years. Yerkes, therefore, doled out bribes, or "boodle money," to the aldermen, but the bill failed. Two aldermen rejected Yerkes's cash, and the transit mogul was ruined. These aldermen were the near-legendary Michael "Hinky Dink" Kenna (1857–1946) and John "Bathhouse" Coughlin (1860–1938). They were not unwilling to accept a little boodle money now and then, but this was too much. Bathhouse quoted advice he received from a mentor: "Keep clear of the big stuff. It's dangerous. Stick to the small stuff; there's little risk, and in the long run, it pays a damned sight more."

In those days, each Chicago ward had two aldermen—not one, as there is today—and Hinky Dink (so-called because of his short stature) and Bathhouse John (he had worked as a masseur in his youth) were the First Ward aldermen for many years. Along with Johnny Powers (also known as Johnny de Pow) of the Nineteenth Ward, they led the council faction known as the "gray wolves," who were notorious for trading votes for cash and other favors. As related in *Lords of the Levee* by Lloyd Wendt and Herman Kogan, Kenna and Coughlin were also known as the "Lords of the Levee." The Levee was Chicago's vice district, a warren of brothels, sleazy taverns, gambling lairs and "dope houses." It was first centered on Custom House

Alderman Michael "Hinky Dink" Kenna's badge. *Chicago History Museum, ICHi-067241.*

Place (now South Federal Street) in the South Loop, but Mayor Carter Harrison Jr. ordered police to clean it up, and it was relocated to the area east of Clark Street between Eighteenth and Twenty-Second Streets. Both districts were part of the First Ward, and Kenna and Coughlin made sure the illegal establishments went unmolested. The pair collected "fees" from proprietors and used the cash to pay off policemen and judges and hire lawyers while keeping commissions for their efforts. From 1896 to 1908, Kenna and Coughlin hosted the scandalous First Ward Ball, a rowdy fundraising event that attracted as many as fifteen thousand revelers—a motley crowd of gamblers, politicians, police captains, business executives, freeloaders, drunks and Levee madams, who brought their "girls" dressed in seductive costumes. Affairs like the ball ensured Hinky Dink and Bathhouse's popularity and kept them in office.

As historian Robin Einhorn put it in *The Encyclopedia of Chicago*, "Chicago voters…are famous for tolerating a certain amount of political corruption in the nineteenth century and most of the twentieth. There is more to this than the city's legendary 'machine politics.' Sometimes it seems corruption is tolerated for its sheer entertainment value." Bathhouse and Hinky Dink are the most memorable examples of this corruption, but they did have a philanthropic and benevolent side. They found jobs for constituents, aided families in financial straits and fed the hungry. When Kenna opened his new saloon, the Workingman's Exchange, in 1903, the *Chicago Tribune* was there:

> In the opposite side of the room is a lunch counter, where bowls of soup… with unlimited quantities of bread are always ready for the hungry. There are no larger receptacles made for beer than the glasses that are handed across the bar. The bowl seems as large as an ordinary hat. The price is 5 cents.…Above the "barrel house" a lodging house is being made ready. There will be rooms for 250 men.…Private lockers, shower baths, iron bedsteads, are some of the conveniences. It is not for the one-night lodger, as the rooms are to be rented by the week. The rate will be $1 each. "I am going to give these poor 'hobos' the best home they ever had in their lives," said Ald. Kenna.

In 1893, British journalist William Stead came to Chicago, took a room above a Levee saloon, studied the situation and, a year later, published *If Christ Came to Chicago*, one of the most probing and critical analyses of the city ever made. Stead had arrived just as the depression of 1893 was afflicting Chicago, and he witnessed the desperation of the unemployed and the homeless. Stead was harsh on the city's upper classes, especially the millionaire "Chicago Trinity" of Marshall Field, George Pullman and Philip Armour, for refusing aid to the poor on the grounds that "coddling" them encouraged idleness. But Stead praised the saloonkeepers and ward politicians for helping, and Kenna was one of those he singled out for providing free lunches. In Stead's opinion, the Democratic Party was "doing the work which the churches ought to do." His efforts to help Chicago's working class were some of the major reasons Kenna's admirers presented him with the solid-gold, diamond-studded badge seen here in 1897.

Kenna and Coughlin remain two of Chicago's most remembered figures— representatives of the city's past and present contradictions. Kenna bequeathed to the city a memorable description, one worthy of being printed on T-shirts and coffee mugs: "Chicago ain't no sissy town."

18.
SEARS, ROEBUCK AND CO. MAILING BOX

Today, online shopping makes it possible for people to buy all sorts of things without leaving home. They are able to look through a large list of options, place an order, and within days, a package arrives at their door. It sounds revolutionary, but you could have done almost the same thing 120 years ago. The merchandise was not sold online, of course; it was sold in a 1,200-page catalog, and orders were placed by mail. Still, shoppers didn't have to leave their houses, and packages soon arrived at their doors. The retail revolution that made such a transaction possible was begun by two Chicago-based firms: Montgomery Ward and Sears, Roebuck and Company. Ward was the first; Sears was the largest.

Aaron Montgomery Ward was born in New Jersey in 1844, and his family moved to Michigan when he was nine. At the age of twenty-one, Ward went to Chicago, where he worked in a department store before deciding to try his luck as a traveling salesman. At the time, farmers, who were distant from urban emporiums, patronized local general stores, where the prices were high and customer satisfaction was beside the point. Ward got the idea of undercutting these stores by selling to farmers by mail. The mail was carried by railroads, and Chicago, the railroad capital, was the perfect distribution center. Ward launched his business in 1871, just in time for the Chicago Fire to destroy his merchandise, but he recovered, and his first bound catalog of thirty-two pages, aimed at a rural clientele, appeared in 1874. Perhaps his most radical idea was a money-back guarantee with no questions asked. With Ward, customer satisfaction *was* the point. His

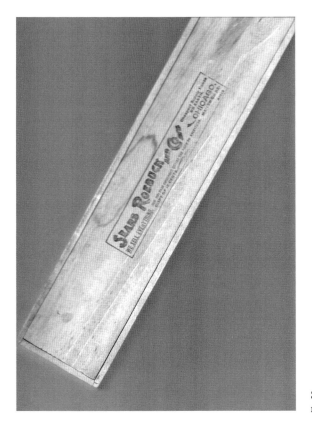

Sears, Roebuck & Co.
mailing box. *Author's collection.*

firm so prospered that, in 1899, he put up the tallest building in Chicago: a twenty-one-story tower on Michigan Avenue. That building has since lost its tower, but the giant complex Ward later built on West Chicago Avenue still has its tower. *The Spirit of Progress*, the bronze sculpture at its pinnacle, is now a beloved local landmark.

When Ward sent out his first catalog in 1874, Richard Warren Sears was all of ten years old. At the age of fourteen, when his father died, he went to work first as a railroad telegrapher and then as a manager of a railroad station, where he began selling discount watches to railroad men. Sears moved to Minneapolis and opened the R.W. Sears Watch Company, but he relocated to Chicago because of its more central location. There, he hired a watch repairman named Alvah Curtis Roebuck, and the pair began selling a variety of merchandise. Sears, Roebuck and Company was incorporated in 1893, the year of its first catalog, which offered a remarkable variety of items, including musical instruments, baby carriages, saddles, bicycles, guns—the list goes on. Eventually, Sears sold everything from A (abdominal bands) to

Z (Zylonite rugs), including prefab kit houses, and the "Big Book," or "Wish Book" (Sears wrote the entire thing), became, as Sears put it, "your right arm to reach out and touch the world." Sears's advertising budget was enormous, and it took him only seven years to surpass Ward in sales. Roebuck couldn't take the pace and cashed out in 1895. His replacement, Julius Rosenwald, eventually became one of the nation's great philanthropists. He created a fund that built more than five thousand schools in the South for Black children, and in Chicago, he financed the Museum of Science and Industry.

By 1906, Sears had annual sales of $50 million and nine thousand employees and had opened a massive distribution center on the West Side. When Sears died in 1914, Rosenwald took over. In the 1920s, the company began focusing on retail stores, and by 1932, retail sales were greater than catalog sales. By the early 1970s, Sears, with over eight hundred stores nationwide, was the largest retailer in the United States. By 1989, the catalog had become unprofitable; it was discontinued in 1993. The Sears stores struggled on but found it increasingly difficult to compete with newer retailers like Walmart and Target. Montgomery Ward closed its last remaining stores in 2001.

The stores are mostly gone, but Sears and Ward bequeathed Chicago enduring and esteemed monuments. One is as obvious as could be; the other, not so much—or at least not in the same way. In 1974, Sears put up what was then the world's tallest building, the 110-story Sears Tower. Its distinctive profile is what architect Bruce Graham described as a "bundled tube" of nine column-free squares that rise to varying heights until only two remain at the pinnacle. In 2009, the British insurance company Willis Group Holdings Ltd. agreed to lease 140,000 square feet of space if the building would be renamed Willis Tower. So, it was—though it's debatable how many Chicagoans use that name. As for Aaron Montgomery Ward, in 1893, the same year Sears was incorporated, he invited a group of Michigan Avenue property owners to his office to propose the creation of a park in the area on the east side of the street, which was then a jumble of city buildings, shacks, stables and piles of junk. It took him years to fight developers who wanted to build on the land, but in the end, he prevailed. Ward's contribution doesn't have his name on it, but maybe Grant Park should be Ward Park.

19

SKINNING KNIVES SET FROM THE CHICAGO STOCKYARDS

For a greater part of Chicago's history, the city's main tourist attraction was not the Art Institute or the Magnificent Mile; it was a grim complex of slaughterhouses on the West Side. At the Union Stock Yard, visitors, led by guides along catwalks, could watch a living, squealing animal be killed and dismantled in minutes, about six hundred in an hour, producing a foul and unforgettable odor and a river of blood. Sightseers came away both impressed and depressed by what historian Dominic A. Pacyga, in his book *Slaughterhouse; Chicago's Union Stock Yard and the World It Made*, termed "industrialized death." Upton Sinclair, the author of the famed packinghouse exposé *The Jungle* (1905), commented, "One could not stand and watch very long without becoming philosophical."

As the country's railroad capital, Chicago was well positioned to become "hog butcher to the world," as poet Carl Sandburg called it. The cattle, hogs and sheep raised in the West and Midwest could be carried in railcars to the Windy City to be driven into pens, sold, butchered and then shipped as packaged goods to the East and overseas. In all, it's estimated that, during the life of the Chicago packinghouses, one billion animals passed through the city. All sorts of byproducts were extracted: fertilizer, buttons, brush bristles, candles, bone meal, soap, wool, glue, medications, violin strings and more. In 1892, an observer remarked, "In a modern packinghouse, nothing is lost of a hog but the squeal and the curl in the tail."

Chicago's first slaughterhouse opened in 1827; the animals were driven in on foot. Several small packinghouses followed, and railroads

Skinning knives set from the Chicago stockyards. *Gift of Lawrence Trickle to the Packingtown Museum, Chicago.*

began bringing in livestock in the 1850s. Having stockyards scattered in various parts of the city proved inefficient, especially when it involved transferring animals from one yard to another by parading them down city streets. A coalition of businessmen prevailed on the governor to sign a law authorizing the construction of a centralized market on Halsted and Forty-Third Streets in what was then a suburban community called Town of Lake. The stockyard opened on Christmas Day in 1865, and the first hogs arrived the following morning.

The Union Stock Yard became not just a collection of animal pens and slaughterhouses but also an out-and-out city. It had a police force, fire department, electric plant, bank, racetrack, beltline railroad and stop on the "El." The Transit House Hotel provided deluxe accommodations for visiting shippers and, occasionally, their wives. After the hotel burned down during a huge stockyard fire in 1910, it was replaced by the Stock Yard Inn, where diners selected their own steaks and branded their initials into the meat with a hot iron in the Sirloin Room. The threat of fire was a constant. Fires broke out in 1866, 1873, 1897 and 1899; the 1910 fire killed twenty-one firemen (the most in a single incident in Chicago history), and the fire in 1934 destroyed dozens of major structures and scores of workers' homes.

The leading meatpackers were known as the Big Six: Armour, Swift, Morris, National Packing, Cudahy and S&S (Schwarzschild and Sulzberger, later Wilson). By the 1920s, Armour, Swift and Wilson had come to dominate the industry. The area that grew up around the stockyard was known as "Packingtown," a realm of workers' cottages, small tenements and plentiful saloons and churches, each catering to a specific ethnic group. Over it all hung the rank odor known as the "Bridgeport smell." The disassembly line in the packinghouses moved with a frightening speed through dark, unventilated, unheated workrooms, and the workers (some of them children) were subject to skin infections, respiratory diseases and rheumatism, all while fending off the flying roaches known as "bombers." Chicago's reputation as being the heart of American organized labor was earned by the stockyard workers, who formed unions and regularly went on strike. Wages were always an issue, and the eight-hour workday was a contentious subject for decades. One union member was killed during a violent thirteen-week walkout in 1948 that ended in defeat and a backlash

The Union Stock Yard in 1941. *Library of Congress.*

against what was perceived as the union's leftist leadership. But despite the hardships and agitation, many workers used their jobs as the first rung on a ladder that eventually enabled them to move out of Packingtown, allowing their children to go on to better jobs and careers.

The Union Stock Yard peaked in 1924 and then began to decline. Packinghouses began to open in other states as farmers came to prefer selling to markets closer to them; even Chicago packers established plants west of the Mississippi. It became more common for meatpackers to buy directly from suppliers, cutting out the central position of the Chicago livestock pens, and the packers began to view the city's pro-union bias as a liability and sought out states with antiunion laws. Finally, the increasing use of trucks for shipping, facilitated by highway construction and improvement, rendered Chicago's position as a rail center less important. By the 1960s, civic leaders had come to feel that slaughterhouses did not fit the image of a modern, progressive, global city. The Union Stock Yard closed on July 31, 1971, and demolition commenced the next day.

20.

PULLMAN PORTER CAP

George Pullman (1831–1897), the man whose name became synonymous with railroad sleeping cars, didn't actually invent them. As early as 1838, the Cumberland Valley Railroad offered sleeping car service, but the beds were cast iron, had no sheets and were stacked in tiers of three. Pullman perfected the car, publicized it, bought out competitors, built a huge factory and achieved a virtual monopoly.

When Pullman came to Chicago in 1855, the city was jacking up its buildings above street level (see "Water Tower Pewter Souvenir"). Pullman, using techniques he had mastered in upstate New York, became an expert structure raiser. He then turned his attention to sleeping cars and realized quality was the secret. His first sleepers debuted in 1859 and were an instant success. Pullman's Pioneer car of 1865 set an even higher standard of rail travel luxury with its thick carpets, cushioned chairs, velvet curtains and chandeliers. When a sleeper car was coupled to another Pullman innovation, the dining car, it was like a hotel on wheels.

In the 1880s, Pullman built his sleeping car factory on Chicago's far South Side. Intending to create an orderly community with no saloons, cheap theaters or other distractions, he put up what he considered wholesome workers' housing. The workers would rent—not buy—the homes (and Pullman would make a profit). The utopian town became a tourist attraction; although not everyone was impressed. Journalist Richard Ely considered it a "gilded cage as a substitute for personal liberty" and branded it "un-American" and a display of "feudalism."

Pullman porter cap. *Smithsonian National Museum of African American History and Culture.*

Pullman's business nosedived during the depression of 1893. He slashed salaries by 20 to 35 percent and then cut hours, which lowered wages even more. But he didn't reduce rents, which were still deducted from paychecks; one employee, it was reported, received a check for two cents (he didn't bother to cash it). Pullman, while still paying dividends to stockholders, obstinately refused to negotiate, and in 1894, the workers walked off the job. When the "Chicago Strike" was taken up by the American Railway Union (ARU), which had been founded in 1893 by Eugene V. Debs, a prominent leftist politician and labor leader, it went national. The ARU initiated a countrywide boycott of Pullman cars, violence on the railroads spread as far as California and the "Debs rebellion" turned into one of the greatest clashes of management and labor in U.S. history. President Grover Cleveland ordered federal troops to Chicago. They arrived on July 4, 1894, and the next day, a mob took over the railroads at the Union Stock Yard and forced the soldiers and police to scatter. More troops were sent in, as well as the state militia, and on July 19, Debs and the strikers capitulated. Pullman had won, but the once-revered entrepreneur was now one of the most hated men in America. His health collapsed, and when he died just three years later, he was entombed under a pile of concrete to prevent militants from vandalizing his grave. In 1898, the Illinois Supreme Court ordered the Pullman Company to sell the housing to the workers, and the "ideal community" was history.

Sleeping cars needed attendants to make up the beds, keep things clean and attend to passengers' needs, and Pullman decided early on that freed enslaved people would be ideal. As Larry Tye explained in *Rising from the Rails: Pullman Porters and the Making of the Black Middle Class,* "They came cheap, and men used to slave labor could be compelled to do whatever work they were asked, for as many hours as told." Pullman hired more Black men than any other employer in the country. Despite their menial status, the porters, who numbered 12,300 at their peak, prized their jobs, and many were able to give their children a college education. In African American communities, porters were personifications of gentility and refinement. The silver "Pullman Porter" emblem on their caps was a badge of honor, and,

An 1893 Pullman sleeper. *Wikimedia Commons.*

in Tye's description, it "had to sparkle." But although 44 percent of the Pullman workforce consisted of porters, they received just 27 percent of the payroll. Their hours were long, days off were few and tips were crucial to supplement meager salaries. Attempts to unionize began around 1900, but given the Pullman Company's fierce anti-labor position, they got nowhere until 1925, when, at a meeting in New York City, the socialist and journalist A. Philip Randolph founded the Brotherhood of Sleeping Car Porters,

The Pullman Factory in 1885. *Library of Congress.*

the first African American labor union. The most militant local union was, naturally, the one in Chicago, headed by the no-nonsense Milton P. Webster. Success didn't come, however, until pro-labor legislation, passed as part of President Franklin Roosevelt's New Deal, forced the Pullman Company to reach a historic agreement with the Brotherhood in 1937.

By the mid-twentieth century, airplanes, buses and private automobiles had made sleeping cars obsolete. The factory closed in 1955, and Pullman ended its sleeping car service in 1969. Most of the buildings survived, however, and the town had a second life when it was designated as a national monument in 2015. When President Barack Obama dedicated it, he said, "This site is at the heart of what would become America's labor movement and, as a consequence, at the heart of what would become America's middle class."

21.

STEEL MILL POSTAGE STAMP

O n New Year's Day in 1913, the U.S. government issued new stamps for the prepayment of fourth-class mail parcel postage—the only parcel post stamps ever issued by the Postal Service, which makes them highly collectible. Among the twelve designs are a mail train, a biplane in flight, a dairy farm, a Florida orange grove and, to represent heavy industry, the South Works of U.S. Steel in Chicago. For much of the twentieth century, steelmaking and meatpacking were the two industries most identified with Chicago. When this stamp was released, the South Works employed about eleven thousand workers. During World War II, it employed twenty thousand and was the biggest employer in the Windy City. The history of Chicago can't be told without the history of steel.

Chicago's first iron and steel companies, like so many other businesses, owed their existence to the railroads. They began by making rails for train tracks; the North Chicago Rolling Mill Company, the city's first rail manufacturing plant, opened in 1857. After the Civil War, the railroads extended to the Calumet River area of Chicago. Congress appropriated funds for a harbor, and the region, which then had access to both lake and rail transportation, quickly became an industrial powerhouse. Four major steel mills were established—first, Wisconsin Steel (originally Joseph H. Brown Iron & Steel) in South Deering and then U.S. Steel South Works (South Chicago), Republic Steel (East Side) and Pressed Steel (Hegewisch). The Calumet River mills became instrumental in the building of modern Chicago by producing the steel skeletons for the city's skyscrapers. A

Above and opposite: Steel mill postage stamp. *Author's collection.*

spokesman for U.S. Steel once said, "Take the buildings out of Chicago that South Works built, and you've got a cow town on your hands." Huge steel mills were also opened nearby in Indiana—U.S. Steel in Gary and Inland Steel and Youngstown Sheet and Tube in Indiana Harbor.

Given Chicago's prominence in the American labor movement, it's not surprising clashes between management and workers became frequent in the city's steel industry. Attempts to unionize steelworkers began in the 1860s. When the American Federation of Labor tried to create a national union of iron- and steelworkers early in the twentieth century, labor actions were numerous. The Great Steel Strike of 1919 was nationwide, but the largest group of workers (some ninety thousand) to walk off the job were Chicagoans. The strike failed, and union activism receded during the 1920s, only to come roaring back with the Great Depression of the 1930s. By early 1937, strikes were rampant in enterprises from rubber factories to the taxi business, hosiery mills and more.

The "police riot" at the 1968 Democratic Convention in Chicago (see "Chicago Police Officer's Riot Helmet") is well-remembered, but the police riot at Chicago's Republic Steel in 1937 has been strangely forgotten. As recounted in *The 1937 Chicago Steel Strike: Blood on the Prairie* by John F. Hogan, in early 1937, U.S. Steel (also known as "Big Steel") signed an agreement

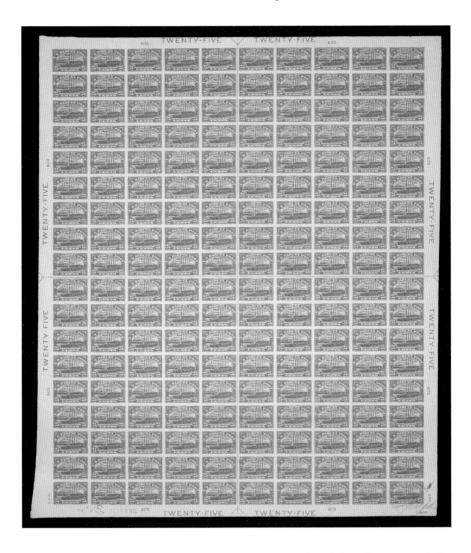

with the Steelworkers Organizing Committee (SWOC). Encouraged by this victory, the SWOC turned its attention to "Little Steel" (Republic, Bethlehem, Inland, Youngstown and Jones & Laughlin, or J&L). After a brief and successful strike against J&L, the SWOC moved on to Republic, which operated a large mill along the Calumet River at 118th Street. Republic said it had no intention of signing a contract, and on May 26, the strike began (strikes were also called at Inland Steel and Youngstown). The strikers used a former tavern/dance hall on South Green Bay Avenue called Sam's Place as a meeting hall, and it was there, on the morning of May 30, that they assembled to march on the mill and set up a picket line. They were met by a formation of some 150 Chicago police officers who launched tear gas bombs, battered strikers with clubs and opened fire, killing ten marchers and injuring 90 others. The strike collapsed, and the workers went back to work, although Republic did eventually sign a contract—five years later. A U.S. Senate investigation, using alarming newsreel footage, determined that all of those who had been killed had been shot in the back or side and that the police had used "excessive force." Public sympathy, at first on the side of the police, pivoted to favor the strikers and, indeed, the entire labor movement.

During World War II, Chicago steel mills operated at 100 percent capacity (Republic even opened a new mill), and by the war's end, American mills were making more than half of all the steel in the world. But the American steel industry, hurt by foreign competition and the failure of owners to modernize many of the mills, declined severely in the 1970s and 1980s. The mill on this stamp closed in 1992, at which time, it employed only 730 people. Republic Steel shuttered its Chicago plant in 2001. A massacre memorial sculpture made by former Republic Steel employee Ed Blazak now stands at the corner of 117th Street and Avenue O. It's made of "100% steel."

22.

EDELWEISS BEER PROMOTIONAL FAN

Chicago is a beer town and has been since the start. Chicago was incorporated in 1833, and the city's first brewery opened in the very same year. In the following decades, the fortunes of Chicago's brewing industry rose and fell, surviving anti-immigrant hostility, Prohibition, the onslaught of corporate brewmonsters and, at one point, the complete disappearance of Chicago-based brewing.

William Lill and Michael Diversey purchased the 1833 brewery, and their popular Lill's Cream Ale was sold as far away as New York and New Orleans. As the number of German immigrants grew, so did beer production. The number of saloons also grew, and a great majority of them were owned by German and Irish immigrants—to the dismay of nativists. Many reformers espoused Sabbatarianism—the doctrine that work, commerce, entertainment, sports and alcohol should be forbidden on Sunday. This policy had a clear anti-immigrant tone. Immigrants, mostly Roman Catholic, guarded traditions of imbibing on Sunday—beer for Germans, whisky for the Irish and (later) wine for Italians—and they saw Sunday "blue laws" as attempts at suppression. When Mayor Levi Boone of the anti-immigrant Know Nothing Party attempted to compel Sunday closings by arresting uncooperative tavern owners and raising the cost of a liquor license to $300, the result was the Lager Beer Riot of 1855, in which protestors charged the downtown area. One person died and dozens were arrested. Although the Sunday closing laws remained, they were almost entirely ignored. After the Chicago Fire, however, the city experienced a

Edelweiss Beer promotional fan. *Author's collection.*

crime wave, and reformers determined it was essential to enforce the Sunday bans. This time, the immigrants turned to the ballot box. The overwhelming victory of pro-liquor Harvey Doolittle Colvin in the mayoral election of 1873 settled the matter and ended Sunday closings.

The Great Fire, however, had destroyed several of Chicago's largest breweries, and German-born brewing titans in Milwaukee and St. Louis, such as Schlitz, Pabst and Busch, rushed in (former Schlitz "tied houses," marked by a distinctive logo, can still be found around Chicago). Still, Chicago's beer makers endured. In 1880, Chicago was pumping out 800,000 barrels, and by 1900, the city boasted some sixty breweries. One of the largest was Conrad Seipp, which, by 1900, was producing 250,000 barrels a year. Around that time, the Peter Schoenhofen Brewing Company opened a huge operation in the Pilsen neighborhood. Its most popular product was Edelweiss, the beer advertised on this delightful fan. The Ostenrieder Advertising Agency invented an assortment of puppet-like "toy boys" to push Schoenhofen's most popular brew. There were about twenty of these cute guys in addition to this determined golfer. Ironically, this fan appeared just months before Prohibition became law on January 17, 1920.

Prohibition, of course, didn't end beer making in Chicago. A few established firms managed to hang on—Schoenhofen made "near beer" and developed the popular Green River soda pop—but the production of real beer went underground. As historian John J. Binder explained in *Al Capone's Beer Wars: A Complete History of Organized Crime in Chicago During Prohibition*, Al Capone said the real money to be made was not from bootlegging spirits but beer. In 1930, the *Chicago Daily News* estimated illegal beer sales brought in $103 million annually, and hard liquor only brought in $56 million. The crime busting "Untouchable" Eliot Ness specialized in raiding Capone's breweries and once even captured the gang boss's master brewer.

The end of Prohibition in 1933, however, did not mean the revival of Chicago brewing. At first, the city's breweries rebounded, but eventually, the Milwaukee/St. Louis behemoths outspent them in advertising. Meanwhile, operating costs rose, and the attachment Chicago drinkers had for their local suds waned. The rock bottom was the closing of the Peter Hand Brewery in 1978; it had been founded in 1891 and made the popular Meister Bräu brand. After it closed, Chicago had exactly zero breweries.

But then, like a desert touched by rain, sprouts began to spring from the dry earth. Brewpubs began appearing in the late 1980s and quickly became popular and widespread. These establishments were generally quite small, but when the Lagunitas Brewing Company of California opened an operation in Chicago in 2014, the city again possessed a major player in the business. By the second decade of the twenty-first century, a woodland of brewing establishments had grown up in the Windy City. In 2018, the Brewers Association reported the number of breweries in the Chicago metropolitan area had reached 167—more than any other city in the United States.

23.

THEODORE THOMAS
MEMORIAL ARRANGEMENT

Chicago sports fans want their local teams to be number one, the best. They're usually disappointed.

But the Windy City possesses a team of players that, year after year, is arguably the best—not just in the country, but in the world. These are the over one hundred players who make up the Chicago Symphony Orchestra (CSO).

Chicagoans were hearing classical music concerts as early as 1850. Several Philharmonic Societies came and went, but Chicago was unable to support a full-time orchestra. An orchestra led by German-born Theodore Thomas (1835–1905) first came to Chicago in 1869. This acclaimed touring ensemble regularly visited major American cities, but its finances were insecure, and Thomas disbanded it in 1888. A year later, Chicago businessman Charles Norman Fay ran into Thomas on a New York street. Thomas, Fay said, looked "worn and worried." He asked if Thomas would come to Chicago if he could have a permanent orchestra. Thomas replied, "I would go to Hell if they gave me a permanent orchestra." Fay lined up a group of "guarantors," including Philip Armour, Marshall Field, George M. Pullman and Cyrus McCormick Jr., who pledged to support the new orchestra financially. The program for the first concert, on October 16, 1891, comprised Wagner's "Faust" overture, Beethoven's Fifth Symphony, Tchaikovsky's first piano concerto and the "Hussite" overture by Dvorak.

In its first seasons, the CSO (then called the Chicago Orchestra) played in the Auditorium building. The theater was beautiful, but the four-

Theodore Thomas's memorial arrangement. *Glessner House.*

thousand-seat interior was too vast for Thomas's liking. When a large property on Michigan Avenue known as Leroy Payne's livery stable came up for sale, the CSO's president, Byron Lathorp, grabbed it for $450,000. Daniel Burnham designed the new hall, which opened with a triumphant concert on December 14, 1904. Just three weeks later, Thomas, who then had everything he wanted and who had never missed a concert, died from pneumonia. One of his pallbearers was businessman John Glessner, who had been one of the CSO's guarantors. The Glessner and Thomas families were close, and the conductor's widow, Rose, gave Frances Glessner, John's daughter, this memorial piece framed by Marshall Field's that contains one of the last batons used by Thomas and a palm frond from his funeral flowers (see "Silver Bowl Made by Frances Glessner").

Thomas's assistant, German-born Frederick Stock (1872–1942), stepped up to the helm of the CSO. One way to have a successful orchestra is to have a single conductor direct it for a long time. Stock stayed for thirty-seven years. In 1905, Stock began the tradition of performing at Ravinia Park in the summer, and in 1916, the CSO became the first U.S. symphony orchestra to make a record. Stock's early recordings allow us to travel in time to another era and hear a polished ensemble that has the music in its bones. Today, it's said the glory of the CSO is its mighty brass section; aficionados report that, according to Stock's recordings, that was true as early the 1920s.

In the years after Stock's death, the CSO has had eight musical directors—Désiré Defauw, Artur Rodzinski, Rafael Kubelik, Fritz Reiner,

Jean Martinon, Georg Solti, Daniel Barenboim and Riccardo Muti. Four (Reiner, Solti, Barenboim and Muti) led the orchestra for a decade or more, which brought an enviable stability to the ensemble. Under Reiner, the CSO made recordings that are still available and some of which are considered definitive. It was also Reiner who initiated the Chicago Symphony Chorus, a corps whose quality essentially equals that of the orchestra. The CSO held its first European tour—now a regular and eagerly anticipated event—under Solti, and Barenboim presided over the conversion of Orchestra Hall into today's renovated and expanded Symphony Center. The orchestra has also welcomed an impressive list of guest conductors, beginning in 1904 with Thomas's friend Richard Strauss (the *Chicago Tribune* proudly reported the great composer considered the CSO the best orchestra in the United States). Others have included Edward Elgar, Maurice Ravel, Sergei Prokofiev, Arnold Schoenberg, Paul Hindemith, Sergei Rachmaninoff, Aaron Copland and Leonard Bernstein.

The CSO's position at the top of the orchestral heap is now secure. The rock band U2 currently holds the record for most Grammy Awards won by a pop group, twenty-two. The CSO (as of this writing) has won sixty-two. When the orchestra went to New York in 2011, *New York Times* music critic Allan Kozinn wrote:

> *The main thing a listener wanted from the Chicago Symphony Orchestra's visit to Carnegie Hall this weekend was a sense of how this great ensemble was faring under the baton of Riccardo Muti....From the moment he cued the orchestra's flutes and clarinets, in the opening of Berlioz's 'Symphonie Fantastique,' at the start of the Saturday evening performance, to his final downbeat on the plangent chord that closed Shostakovich's Fifth Symphony, at the end of the Sunday afternoon concert, worries about the state of American orchestras and those who lead them disappeared.*

In 2017, when the CSO visited the West Coast, *Los Angeles Times* music critic Mark Swed was more concise: "Forget the Cubs. The Chicago Symphony can't lose."

24.

JANE ADDAMS'S NOBEL PRIZE

n 1906, Jane Addams of Chicago was called "the only saint America has produced." A decade later, she was called "a foolish, garrulous old woman" and "a bore." What had happened? The world went to war.

Jane Addams (1860–1935) earned her reputation through an institution she founded in Chicago in 1889 called Hull-House. It was a settlement house, the first in America. She was inspired during a visit, with her friend Ellen Gates Starr, to Toynbee Hall, history's first settlement house, which was located in the East End of London. The settlement house movement, which was born in Britain in the 1880s, was formed to aid the poor through housing, childcare, training and education.

Addams was born in Cedarville, a western Illinois farm town. Her father was a millowner, banker, state senator and friend of Abraham Lincoln. Addams came of age in a time when upper-class and middle-class American women, still struggling to gain footholds in the professional world, were being caught up in a fervor of volunteerism and activism, and they found outlets in social work, charitable enterprises, campaigns for women's suffrage and a surging number of women's clubs. On their return from England, Addams and Starr rented a large home that was once owned by real estate developer Charles J. Hull. When Addams moved in, the mansion, which was then a tenement, was in the middle of a slum—just as she wanted it. The population of the area consisted largely of immigrants from Italy, Greece, Poland and Russia (later, an influx of Mexicans was added). These were people whose experiences with governments had been mostly oppressive, and they were wary of authority. But Addams and Starr, who were bent on proving destitution was not the result of low character or indolence but of a lack of opportunity and education, found acceptance. If immigrants struggled to learn English, Hull-House offered English classes. If immigrants had little education, Hull-House offered night classes and Chicago's first kindergarten.

If immigrants had no hot water, Hull-House provided bathing facilities. Hull-House, which grew to encompass thirteen buildings, offered medical care, day care, job training, a library, a savings bank, a theater, a gymnasium, a playground, a swimming pool, art classes and music lessons (jazz giant Benny Goodman got his start there). Within the larger community, Addams investigated sweatshop conditions and got herself appointed as a garbage inspector. By 1900, more than one hundred other settlement houses had opened in the United States.

Addams's other cause was pacifism and the peace movement. In 1892, she joined the Chicago Peace Society, and on a European trip four years later, she met the world's most famous and uncompromising advocate of pacifism, the great Russian novelist Leo Tolstoy. Shortly after World War I began in August 1914, she was elected the head of a new national organization called the Women's Peace Party, and she was later invited to Europe to preside over the first meeting of the Women's International League for Peace and Freedom. Addams became part of a four-woman contingent that visited Europe's capitals in the forlorn hopes of initiating a peace conference. It was on her tour that a German submarine sunk the ocean liner *Lusitania*, an event that roused war fever in the as-yet-neutral United States. It was at this time that she became the target of militarists in both America and Europe. The *Louisville Courier-Journal* called her "a foolish, garrulous old woman," while *New York Topics* chimed, calling her a "silly, vain, impertinent old maid," and a woman's club newspaper added, "Jane Addams is losing her grip. She is becoming a bore." When the United States entered the war in April 1917, Addams was careful not to criticize the government—although she supported conscientious objectors. After the war, pacifism became popular again. Addams became a regular correspondent with Mohandas Gandhi, Tolstoy's successor as the conscience of pacifism, but she was unable to meet him on her trip to India because he was in prison at the time.

Opposite: Jane Addams's Nobel Prize. *Jane Addams Hull-House Museum.*

Above: Jane Addams in 1914. *Library of Congress.*

In 1931, Addams was awarded the Nobel Peace Prize, seen here on display at the Hull-House Museum. At the presentation ceremony in Oslo, which she was too ill to attend, presenter Halvdan Koht said:

> *In honoring Jane Addams, we also pay tribute to the work which women can do for peace and fraternity among nations....Whenever women have organized, they have always included the cause of peace in their program. And Jane Addams combines all the best feminine qualities which will help us to develop peace on earth....Sometimes, her views were at odds with public opinion both at home and abroad. But she never gave in, and in the end, she regained the place of honor she had had before in the hearts of her people.*

In 2017, Chicago's Hard Rock Hotel, located in the historic Art Deco Carbide & Carbon Building, was sold to new owners. The following year, they reopened it and named it—in honor of Addams—the St. Jane. Sadly, the pandemic of 2020 forced the St. Jane Hotel to close, but in a little over a century, Jane Addams had gone from being an American saint to being an impertinent old maid and then back to being a saint again.

25.
BRYANT WASHBURN
SOUVENIR PLATE

Sometimes, a false historical narrative gets so embedded that no amount of correction seems to dispel it. So it is with the prevailing account of U.S. cinema history, which begins with Thomas Edison's invention of motion pictures, continues with his production of movies in his New Jersey studio, goes on to describe New York nickelodeons and the Vitagraph Company of Brooklyn and then explains how the business relocated to sunny California. In recent years, however, historians have been researching early filmmaking in Chicago and have determined that, for at least ten years, Chicago—not New York or Hollywood—was the movie capital of the United States. The crucial figures of the Chicago film scene were Colonel William Selig, Gilbert M. "Broncho Billy" Anderson and George K. Spoor.

William Selig, born in Chicago in 1864, was an itinerant showman, dabbling in magic, minstrel shows and seances. Then he encountered Edison's Kinetoscope in Dallas and immediately saw the potential of motion pictures. Once back in Chicago, he founded the Selig Polyscope Company. Its studio covered several city blocks, and by 1915, it was said to be the largest movie studio in the world. Selig's star was Tom Mix, the first movie cowboy hero. Selig made the first cliff-hanger serial (*The Adventures of Kathlyn*, 1913–1914), the first film version of *The Wonderful Wizard of Oz* (1910) and *Dr. Jekyll and Mr. Hyde* (1908), probably America's first horror movie. Selig began scouting locations in California not only for its sunshine, but also for the diversity of the terrain, which was suitable for different types of movies.

Bryant Washburn souvenir plate.
Author's collection.

In 1909, he opened, in the Edendale section of Los Angeles, the first movie studio in California, which made him known as "the man who invented Hollywood." Eventually, that studio was making most of Polyscope's story films, while the Chicago operation concentrated on newsreels.

At the turn of the twentieth century, Gilbert Anderson, born Maxwell H. Aronson in Little Rock, Arkansas, in 1880, was working in New York vaudeville and theater. There, he met Edwin S. Porter, who was making films for Edison, and Porter cast him in *The Great Train Robbery* (1903), the first hit narrative film; it was a colossal success. In 1906, Anderson moved to Chicago to work for Selig, who gave him the chance to both act and direct. Anderson soon quit over money disputes and teamed up with George K. Spoor, an entrepreneur who had been experimenting with films and projectors for more than a decade. They named their enterprise Peerless Film Manufacturing Company but changed it to Essanay (that is, S&A, for their initials). Their first star was cross-eyed Ben Turpin, whose popular comedies paid the bills for the first couple of years. Essanay went on to make some two thousand films over the next decade, including the first presidential biopic (*The Life of Abraham Lincoln*, 1908), the first film version of *A Christmas Carol* (1908), and the first "pie in the face" gag (*Mr. Flip*, 1909). Essanay's *Sherlock Holmes* (1916), the first American film featuring the British sleuth, was lost for ninety-eight years until it was rediscovered in France in 2014. Essanay's roster included such future stars as Harold Lloyd, Gloria Swanson and Wallace Beery. Its biggest catch was Charlie Chaplin, but Chaplin stayed in Chicago for less than a month (he hated the cold), made just one film (*His New Job*, which has survived) and quarreled over what he saw as the studio's poor artistic standards. Another Essanay star was Bryant Washburn, whose handsome visage was printed onto this souvenir plate. He played villains at first but soon showed a comedic gift. Washburn was then eclipsed by Essanay's Francis X. Bushman, who is usually considered the first movie matinee idol. Anderson, himself, then known as "Broncho Billy," specialized in westerns, which were extremely popular, and the need for authentic locations drew Essanay to California shortly after Selig made the move. Not only was California's weather better, but it was also increasingly difficult to find the expansive spaces needed for ever more ambitious pictures in crowded Chicago.

Today, only a few reminders of Chicago's cinematic glory exist. An apartment building at 3900 North Claremont Street has an "S" inside a diamond over its entry, indicating it was once part of the Selig empire. The Essanay Studios building at 1345 West Argyle Street was landmarked in 1996 and still sports the studio name and logo. It's now part of St. Augustine College.

The studios are gone, but—one might think—at least we have the movies. Unfortunately, we don't; it's estimated that only about 1 percent of the movies that were made during this era survive.

26

ILLINOIS CENTRAL TIMETABLE

For thousands of African Americans, this object was not just a railroad timetable but also a passport to freedom, a ticket to opportunity, a "get out of jail free" card. Historian Isabel Wilkerson has called the Illinois Central Railroad (IC) "the Overground Railroad for slavery's grandchildren." The IC was a great river of steel that carried them from the South to Chicago. This timetable dates back to 1912, two years before World War I, an event that opened up jobs in Chicago and other northern cities. Job opportunities were a major reason for what is known as the "Great Migration." In just two years (1916–1918), the Black population of Chicago doubled, and before the migration ended (around 1970), some six million Black people had moved from the South to northern states, and half a million of them moved to Chicago.

Chicago's heavy industries, particularly meatpacking and steel, relied on European immigrants, but the Great War dried up that source just when the warring nations were in dire need of American products. Then, when the United States entered the war in 1917, some four million young Americans entered military service and were removed from farms and factories. Not only were Black people in the South willing to replace them, but they also had strong incentives to leave the South. Their voting rights hardly existed, schools and housing were terrible and the sickening ritual of lynching, in which a mob would hang a Black man (sometimes a woman) for trivial—or nonexistent—infractions, was extensive.

This page and next: Illinois Central timetable. *Author's collection.*

At that time, railroad service was available to an extent that is almost unimaginable today, and the maps inside this timetable are a revelation. In Mississippi, for example, railroad stations with Chicago connections were *everywhere*. Fares were affordable, but when the IC itself started to feel the labor pinch, it carried laborers to Chicago at no charge. News of opportunities in the Windy City were carried to the South on the IC by Pullman porters (see "Pullman Porter Cap"), many of whom would bring the *Chicago Defender*, the country's largest Black-owned newspaper. In many editorials, it implored Black southerners to come north. In May 1917, the *Defender* launched an emigration initiative called the "Great Northern Drive." A year later, the newspaper reported, "They left in droves, are still leaving, and only a few have returned. The effect has been to paralyze the industries of the South, while the other sections of the country have prospered. The experiment proved a success."

The migration startled the solid White citizens of the South, who found their workforce disappearing. An editorial in a Macon, Georgia newspaper put it plainly, "We must have the Negro in the South. It is the only labor we have, it is the best we possibly could have—if we lose it, we go bankrupt!" In his book *Negro Migration During the War* (1920), Black journalist Emmett J. Scott reported the mayor of New Orleans begged the president of the IC to stop carrying Black passengers north. The president replied that, "as common carriers, they could not refuse to sell tickets or to provide the necessary transportation." In 1919, the *Defender* explained, "[The South] wants us and it doesn't want us. The truth is, it wants us as serfs and vassals, but not as men and citizens. The conditions upon which it wants us never will be complied with." In other words, the Great Migration was unstoppable.

When the emigrants reached Chicago, they disembarked at the Illinois Central Depot, a handsome Romanesque Revival structure at Michigan

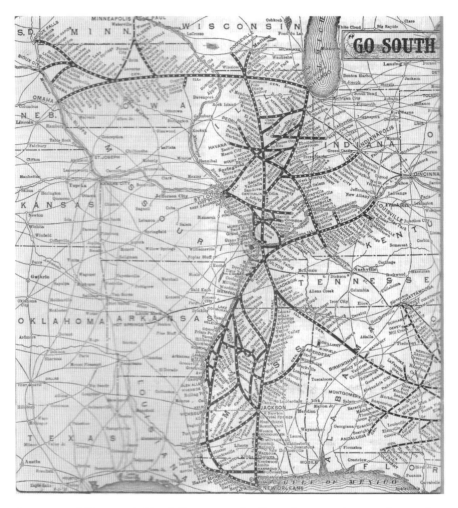

Avenue and Roosevelt Road. It was not far from the area that was becoming known as Bronzeville, the core of Black life in the Windy City. On the stretch of State Street from Twenty-Second Street to Forty-Eighth Street, called the "Stroll," there were dozens of cabarets, nightclubs, theaters and music halls, most of which were owned by African American entrepreneurs. Jazz was everywhere (see "James Palao's Saxophone").

Yet, Chicago was hardly a paradise. Limited housing opportunities led to overcrowding, and African Americans who bought homes in White neighborhoods were often targeted by bombs. Many public facilities were off limits to Black citizens, and between July 27 and August 3, 1919, Chicago was the scene of a violent race riot in which fifteen White people and twenty-three Black people were killed.

Nevertheless, the opportunities in Chicago were undeniable. In 1916, the *Defender* said, "It is a fact that the North holds out a hundred opportunities to every one that the laborer will find in the South. Not alone will he find an abundance of work, but the housing and living conditions are so superior there is no comparison. The wages are so much higher for workers of every kind." That prejudice existed probably did not surprise the Black newcomers, but they were pleasantly surprised to find it was not universal, as it was in the South. For example, Black shoppers were amazed that they were allowed to try on clothing in stores. Perhaps most important, African Americans could vote in Chicago, and it didn't take them long to elect their own representatives. Chicago's first Black alderman was Oscar De Priest, elected in 1915. Thirteen years later, De Priest became the first Black congressman of the modern era.

One small anecdote, however, vividly illustrates the changed atmosphere found in the North. A migrant from Alabama named Charles Denby was traveling northbound on the IC, and when the train crossed the Ohio River into Illinois, Denby, to his astonishment, found himself sitting next to a White passenger. "He was reading a paper," Denby later recalled, "and when he finished half, he pushed it to me and asked if I wanted to read."

27.

WORLD WAR I DOG TAGS

World War II, for most Americans, is the war most prominent in their consciousness. And this is for good reason: the veterans are rapidly dying out, while movies and television are diligently relating their stories. But it can be argued that World War I was the real game-changer for America. Although the Second World War has been called the "Good War," the First World War has been called (by historian G.J. Meyer) the "war that changed everything." Without World War I, there would have been no World War II, no Soviet Russia, no Nazi Germany, no Holocaust, no communist China, no Korean War, no Vietnam War—even the strife in the Middle East can be traced to the war's aftermath, when European diplomats drew national borders with inadequate foresight.

The First World War began in Europe in July 1914; the United States entered the fight in April 1917. The most momentous changes the war made to Chicago were demographic. As recounted in "Illinois Central Timetable," four million men went into military service, and Chicago suffered a worker shortage. First, the job opportunities were a magnet for African Americans in the South and led to the Great Migration. Second, with immigration from Europe slowing to a trickle, employers persuaded Labor Secretary William B. Wilson to relax restrictions on Mexican immigration. The Mexican presence in Chicago, now so powerful, began in this period. The third demographic change was one of reduction. World War I prompted a frenzy of anti-German hysteria. It's not that the German population declined, but many German Americans changed their

World War I dog tags. *Author's collection.*

names and no longer described themselves as German. In 1914, 191,000 Chicagoans identified themselves as German; in 1920, that number had dropped to just 112,000. Finally, as in World War II, the labor shortage drew women into jobs that were once held by men. The thousands of women who came to Chicago for work also found social and sexual freedom, and by the war's end, the "new woman" had arrived.

These dog tags belonged to Stanley Pokorzynski, who is listed on the roster of the 344th Infantry as a musician who formerly lived at 1055 North Ashland Avenue. His surname and his address put him squarely in what's been called Chicago's "Polish Downtown." His last name, Pokorzynski, is as an example of the staggering ethnic variety of the American armed forces. Among the soldiers on the roster of his division are such names as McGonagle, Kotlaba, Libakken, Tortorello, Vartabedian, Papademetrious, Goetzke, Shultis and Duval. It's been estimated that one out of every five U.S. soldiers in the war was born overseas, and 100,000 couldn't speak English. When the war began in Europe, members of Chicago's ethnic communities supported different sides. Many Germans rallied to the Kaiser, while Czechs and Slovaks saw the war as an opportunity to throw off the Austrian rule and win national independence. The Serbs were fiercely anti-German and anti-Austrian, but most Hungarians remained loyal to the Austrian emperor. What was once Poland was divided between Germany, Russia and Austria, and the Poles had to choose which was their enemy. Most came out against Germany, and Chicago's young Poles became eager volunteers, especially after President Woodrow Wilson came out in support of Polish independence. According to historian Dominic A. Pacyga in *American Warsaw*, as many as 300,000 Polish Americans served in the U.S. military and 10,000 were from Chicago.

Most of the soldiers from Chicago, like Stanley Pokorzynski, belonged to the 86th Division, known as the Black Hawk Division, which trained at Camp Grant near Rockford, Illinois. The War Department regularly poached soldiers from this division to fill vacancies elsewhere. As a group, the 86th was not sent to Europe until the war was nearly over, and it never got to go into combat as a unit. Other Chicago soldiers were in the 33rd Division (the "Prairie" Division), a downstate outfit that received transfers from the 86th. This unit endured bloody combat in four major campaigns. All these soldiers were White because the U.S. military was racially segregated, but young Black Chicagoans also did their part. Most of them belonged to the 370th Infantry Regiment, formerly the 8th Regiment of the Illinois National Guard. Although most of the 370,000 Black soldiers who served in the U.S. military were assigned to low-level labor, such as unloading ships, the 370th battled in some of the toughest points of combat of the war—the regiment landed in France with 2,500 men and came back with 1,260. When they returned to Chicago, they were welcomed in a grand parade on Michigan Avenue. In 1927, a memorial to the men of the "Old Eighth" was erected at Thirty-Fifth Street and South Parkway (now Dr. Martin Luther King Jr. Drive). It remains one of the most impressive World War I monuments in the city and is worth a visit.

28.

JAMES PALAO'S SAXOPHONE

n the 1920s, the most popular music in America was jazz, which is why the decade is also known as the Jazz Age, a term invented by novelist F. Scott Fitzgerald in 1922. And the beating heart of the new music was Chicago, the jazz capital of the United States.

Most of the leading jazz musicians performing in Chicago in the 1920s, both White and Black, were from New Orleans. They included Jelly Roll Morton, Manuel Perez, Freddie Keppard, Sidney Bechet, Earl ("Fatha") Hines, Kid Ory, Johnny Dodds, the Original Dixieland Jazz Band (ODJB), Tom Brown and, most notably, King Oliver and Louis Armstrong—more on them later.

A tale commonly told is that New Orleans musicians came to Chicago after the military closed the red-light district known as "Storyville" during World War I, thus putting the jazzmen out of work. This is mostly a myth. First, Storyville's dance halls and saloons remained open, and jazz was still played. Second, the early jazz bands did not commonly play in bordellos; they found work in parades, on riverboats, in vaudeville theaters and at picnics and parties. Third, jazz musicians began leaving New Orleans for Chicago well before World War I. Spencer Williams, the composer of "Basin Street Blues," arrived in Chicago in 1907. The pianist Tony Jackson came around 1912, and Jelly Roll Morton followed in 1914.

In the 1920s, jazz was mostly heard in two areas of Chicago. On South State Street was the "Stroll"—a strip of clubs, cabarets and theaters that was the core of Black entertainment (See "Illinois Central Timetable").

James Palao's saxophone. *Chicago History Museum, ICHi-040409.*

Dreamland, the Savoy Ballroom, the Lincoln Gardens and the Pekin Theater were all located here. White bands played mostly in the Loop, where the clubs included the College Inn, Lamb's Café and the Friar's Inn.

The saxophone seen here belonged to James "Jimmy" Palao of New Orleans (he was a multi-instrumentalist who most often played the violin). Although he is barely mentioned in standard jazz histories, he was an important, unappreciated figure. Born in 1879, he was older than the musicians listed previously and had been present at the birth of jazz. (It was said he taught the art of reading music to the semilegendary Buddy Bolden, perhaps the foundational figure in jazz history.) Palao was, with Bill Johnson, the founder of the Original Creole Orchestra, the first jazz ensemble to leave New Orleans and mount a nationwide tour. Dave Peyton, music columnist for the *Chicago Defender*, the nation's leading Black-owned newspaper, wrote of their debut in Chicago in 1914. "How well do I remember that opening night, and at that time, I predicted that the Creole style of playing music would soon grip the Middle West." Peyton held that the group inspired other New Orleans musicians to go to Chicago. "Their Creole brothers down home, learning of this success, decided to come to the land of the free and plenty money. One by one, they came North, most all of them top-notchers on their instruments." Two of Palao's early business cards still survive. One of them displays the term "Jaz"; the other "Jazz." Both cards have "1908" written on the back. If those years are correct, the standard dating of the origin of the term *jazz* will need to be pushed back several years. Currently, the most common theory is that *jazz* (as applied to music) originated in California around 1915.

The Original Creole Orchestra broke up in 1918, and Palao joined a band led by clarinetist Lawrence Duhé. The cornetist was King Oliver, who soon took over as leader. On a California tour, Oliver and Palao had a falling out. Palao split from the group and went on to play with several other bands while, in 1922, Oliver's men settled in as the house band at Chicago's Lincoln Gardens. Later that year, Oliver summoned from New Orleans his protégé, twenty-two-year-old Louis Armstrong, an event that marks the extraordinary metamorphosis of jazz from a rough-and-ready party music into an art form. Armstrong taught America how to swing, turned jazz into a soloist's art by expanding the concept of improvisation and developed a unique singing style that influenced nearly every subsequent pop singer. The jazz scholar Gary Giddens had called Armstrong America's Bach, and it's not unlikely that he was indeed America's greatest musician.

It was in Chicago in 1925 that Armstrong organized the Hot Fives and the Hot Sevens, groups that made some of the greatest recordings in any style of music. That was the same year Jimmy Palao died. Among the group of mourners who braved the bitter cold at Chicago's Mount Olivet Cemetery for the burial on that January day was Louis Armstrong—the younger generation paying its respects to a founding father.

29.
MEXICAN CERAMIC JUG FROM THE HULL-HOUSE KILNS

In 2019, the American public television show *No Passport Required* aired a program on Chicago's Pilsen neighborhood. As the title suggests, the show's theme was that there are ethnic neighborhoods in American cities where the cultural identity is so strong that visitors might feel they're in a foreign country. In the case of Pilsen, that identity is Mexican. Although gentrification is eroding Pilsen's Hispanic tone, it remains a place where one can readily buy carnitas, piñatas, molcajetes and gowns for a quinceañera. It is also home to the National Museum of Mexican Art. It came as no surprise to inhabitants of the Windy City when food critic José R. Ralat, in his *American Tacos: A History and Guide*, called Chicago a "taco capital."

In 1920, the Mexican population of Chicago was about 1,200. Ten years later, it was 20,000. Today, the Chicagoland region is home to some 1.7 million people of Mexican birth or heritage. Although the numbers are as dramatic as those of the Great Migration of African Americans from the South, the Mexican influx has received less attention from historians. As Ray Hutchinson, a well-known scholar of urban life has put it, "The Mexican community in Chicago may be one of the best-kept secrets in ethnic studies."

In the late nineteenth century, the Mexican government staged a "modernization" campaign that stripped thousands of peasants of their land. That was followed in 1910 by a revolution that threw the nation into turmoil. Then, as related in "World War I Dog Tags," World War I created a labor shortage in the United States, so the federal government relaxed restrictions on Mexican immigration. In Chicago, the first immigrants, the

Mexican ceramic jug from the Hull-House kilns. *Jane Addams Hull-House Museum.*

great majority of whom were male, found work, as did earlier immigrants, in Chicago's heavy industry, especially steel, meatpacking and the railroads. During the Great Steel Strike of 1919, the millowners brought in Mexican laborers as strikebreakers, sometimes sneaking them in undetected.

The Mexican newcomers quickly encountered racial prejudice. They were sometimes characterized as "colored"; landlords denied them housing, some movie theaters restricted them to separate seating, earlier immigrants saw them as competitors for jobs and city officials viewed them as dangers to public health. Such hostility had the effect of inspiring a sense of national identity. Mexicans were far from monolithic; the different states had different cultures, while the civil strife that followed the revolution put Mexicans into different political camps. In Chicago, these factions forged a kind of unity through entities such as mutual aid societies (*mutualistas*), labor unions and political clubs, while pool halls became meeting places where single young men found comradeship and encouragement. A main source of support was the Roman Catholic Church; St. Francis of Assisi Church on Roosevelt Road, originally founded to serve the German community, became the immigrants' spiritual home. There, they found venues for youth groups, literary clubs and performing arts groups.

The first large Mexican neighborhood in Chicago took shape on the Near West Side, which was the site of Hull-House, the settlement house that social worker Jane Addams and Ellen Gates Starr had founded in 1885 (see "Jane Addams's Nobel Prize"). At first, most of the immigrants they served were Italian, Greek, Jewish and Polish, but when the Mexicans came, they reached out to them, too. One of their ventures with this new group was pottery classes, which turned out to be surprisingly successful because many immigrants had come from regions of Mexico with a strong ceramic tradition. The Hull-House Kilns operated from 1927 to 1937, during which time, students produced quite salable plates, jugs, figurines and more (beginning in 1931, Hull-House operated a store on Michigan Avenue). The jug seen here, which went for three dollars, was made by José Ruiz of Hull-House. The swastikas seem discordant today, but the symbol is ancient and was one of seven basic Mexican cultural motifs advocated in an influential book by the Mexican nationalist artist Adolfo Best Maugard.

Largely because of the discord caused by regionalism and civil war, in the 1920s, the Mexican government initiated an effort to forge a national culture by stressing types of rural dance, music, cuisine, art and dress that we now identify as typically Mexican. Hull-House teachers and artists— and even Addams herself—visited Mexico and came away impressed with this initiative, which they promoted when they were back in Chicago. Students in the Hull-House Kilns, for example, were encouraged to focus on Mexican folkloric themes. Because of such efforts, the Mexican anthropologist Manuel Gamio (1883–1960), in two books on Mexican immigration that he published in the early 1930s, argued that it was in the United States, not their homeland, that Chicago's Mexicans acquired a unifying national identity, or what they called their *Mexicanidad*. José Ruiz's pitcher is one of the most attractive results of this effort.

30.

CHICAGO BUNGALOW
STAINED-GLASS WINDOW

Every once in a while, a vintage bungalow in Chicago is demolished, and antique dealers salvage the stained-glass windows. More often, a bungalow owner replaces an old window with a new energy-efficient one, and the old one is rescued. Either way, the recovered widows are very collectible.

It's estimated that about one-third of Chicago's bungalows were built with leaded decorative windows, and the windows were quite affordable (this one probably cost between $2.00 and $4.00 when it was new). According to the Chicago Architecture Foundation's book *The Chicago Bungalow*, an estimated 80,000 and 100,000 bungalows were built in Chicago between 1910 and 1940. That's a lot of glass.

During World War I, working-class Chicago families were typically squeezed into multiple-family dwellings; they were often old one-family houses that had been carved into apartments or dark frame cottages at the back of lots. Gas, electricity and indoor plumbing were not unheard of but were expensive and out of reach for most residents. Things changed in the prosperous 1920s, when an innovative style of housing swept across Chicago—the "bungalow." Tourists seldom see it (except perhaps from a skyscraper observation deck), but a vast sickle-shaped "bungalow belt" took shape to the north, west and south of the center of the city.

Bungalows were considered the embodiment of all the good things that were being brought by a new age of progress and technology. The interiors featured not only decorative glass, but also fireplaces, archways, hardwood

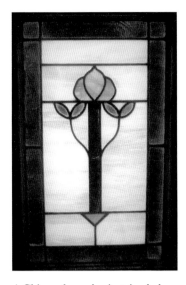

A Chicago bungalow's stained-glass window. *Author's collection.*

floors, built-in bookcases and durable hygienic glazed tiles on the walls and floors of the kitchens and bathrooms. The exterior walls were solid brick, often with carved stone trim. Some design features (wide eaves, an overhanging horizontal roof line, certain art glass motifs) were adapted from Chicago's own Prairie School of Architecture, which had originated with Frank Lloyd Wright. The standard form had five primary rooms on the first floor; the second floor was unfinished but offered the possibility of adding two more rooms. Bungalows usually ranged in size from about 1,200 to 2,400 square feet, which could mean a bedroom for each child and a separate dining room—previously unthinkable luxuries.

Finally, the houses had yards in the front and back and a sheltered entry and sitting porch. In the 1920s, builders recommended twenty-five electrical outlets for every home—more than two per room. Electric appliances became common, and owners could enjoy refrigerators, dishwashers, electric irons, vacuum cleaners, clothes washers, toasters and fans. Natural gas was used for stoves, water heaters and furnaces. Many of the appliances were made in Chicago, like Hotpoint toasters, Streamliner Radios, Sunbeam coffee makers and Hamilton electric calendar clocks. These labor-saving features were marketed as blessings for wives and mothers, and the technology helped create the world's first consumer economy. Improved transportation was an essential factor in the building of the bungalow belt. The streetcar lines were being pushed into the outer neighborhoods; by 1925, Chicago had over 1,300 miles of streetcar track. In 1929, streetcars operated by Chicago Surface Lines (CSL) were carrying nearly 900 million passengers. Finally, automobiles were being used to get to work, and bungalow salesmen were promoting a new feature of the modern home—the garage.

One vital aspect of the bungalow boom is that it brought homeownership to working-class and middle-class buyers. In Chicago, bungalow prices ranged from $2,500 to $10,000; a buyer could move in with $100 down and a monthly mortgage payment of $25, which put bungalows in the price range of a fireman, a teacher or a well-paid factory hand. In short, the Chicago housing market had reached the point at which at least some tenement dwellers could buy a home. Whereas Chicago neighborhoods had once commonly been defined by ethnicity, the bungalow created neighborhoods categorized by economic class.

Today, one out of every three single-family homes in Chicago is a bungalow. Through their decades of ownership, Chicago bungalow owners probably didn't think much more about their homes other than that they were comfortable, convenient and affordable. They must have been surprised, therefore, to discover one day that they were living in historic properties. In 2000, the city, along with the Chicago Architecture Foundation and the Chicago Historic Bungalow Association, launched the Historic Chicago Bungalow Initiative—a marketing, educational and financial project meant to publicize and protect Chicago bungalows. Today, nearly a dozen areas are designated as bungalow historic districts, including Falconer, Wrightwood, Talman West Ridge and Rogers Park Manor. They offer the inquisitive traveler a fresh and unexpected insight into an entirely different aspect of Chicago's famous historic architecture.

31.

PORTABLE RADIO MANUFACTURED BY OPERADIO

During the golden age of radio, from the early 1920s to the mid-1950s, Chicago invented the situation comedy (sitcom), the soap opera and the portable radio—an impressive trio of achievements by any standard.

According to the *Encyclopedia of Chicago*, by the end of the 1920s, about one-third of American radios were being made in the Windy City. There were Hallicrafters, Zenith, General Television & Radio, Westinghouse, Motorola and Operadio, the manufacturer of the object seen here. The Operadio Corporation was founded in 1922 by J. McWilliams ("Mac") Stone. This model was advertised as a "self-contained radio set," and most experts consider it the first modern portable radio. Battery powered, it had an internal horn speaker and a loop antenna inside a folding panel. You had to be fairly fit to take it to the beach (it weighed forty pounds), and the price was also hefty—$190 (about $2,300 today). But it was popular; in the early 1920s, the company reported a three-week backlog of orders.

Chicago's first radio station, KYW, began broadcasting in 1921. WLS was founded three years later by Sears, Roebuck and Company (WLS, or "World's Largest Store"), and other stations followed. In 1924, the *Chicago Tribune* bought radio station WAAF and changed the call letters to WGN ("World's Greatest Newspaper"). By 1925, there were some forty radio stations in Chicagoland.

It was on WGN that history's first sitcom, *Sam 'n' Henry*, premiered on January 12, 1926. It was the creation of two entertainers—Freeman Gosden

A portable radio manufactured by Operadio. *Benson Ford Research Center, the Henry Ford.*

of Richmond, Virginia, and Charles Correll from Peoria, Illinois. It was about two young Black men who migrated to Chicago from the South. Gosden and Correll spoke in what they imagined to be African American dialect, but it was largely derived from the minstrel show. Blackface comedy had been a dominant form of entertainment since the 1830s, but with the advent of radio, a White comic no longer had to put on blackface but could do dialect routines solely with the voice. As the series progressed, characters were added, and although racial stereotypes were inevitable, the characters were generally sympathetic. When Gosden and Correll's contract with WGN expired, they signed with WMAQ. Because WGN still owned *Sam 'n' Henry*, the pair had to invent new characters, and *Amos 'n' Andy* premiered on February 25, 1928. It became the most popular program in the history of broadcasting. In 1928, the U.S. population was about 120 million; *Amos 'n' Andy* attracted 40 million listeners every night. Many African Americans enjoyed it; in 1931, the Black-owned newspaper *Chicago Defender* appointed Gosden and Correll guests of honor at its Bud Billiken Parade. One reason

Black listeners liked *Amos 'n' Andy* was that its humor was not condescending. Amos and Andy had their faults, but they were not cartoons, and many of the show's other characters were successful and admirable. Elizabeth McLeod, writing in *The Original Amos 'n' Andy: Freeman Gosden, Charles Correll and the 1928–1943 Radio Serial*, said the show "not only acknowledged the existence of an educated, prosperous Black middle class, but the new series also made members of that class integral players in the continuing story." *Amos 'n' Andy* remained on the radio until 1960 (in the early 1950s, there was a brief TV series), and it remains a worthwhile topic for examining how America's problematic racial history has intersected with the nation's popular culture.

The first soap opera premiered on WGN on October 20, 1930. It was the creation of Irna Phillips, who was born in Chicago in 1901 and went to Northwestern and the University of Illinois. While teaching school in Ohio, she returned to Chicago for a christening and, almost on a whim, stopped at WGN for an audition. With another actress, she developed a chat show about two women named Sue and Irene, after which, management asked her to create a serial aimed specifically at women. The result was the fifteen-minute serial *Painted Dreams*, the first soap opera. It was about a Chicago-based Irish American family headed by a kindly widow named Mother Moynihan (played by Phillips). The show's other characters included Mother Moynihan's friends; her grown children; her boarder, Sue Morton; and her dog, Mike (also voiced by Phillips). Phillips had a dispute with WGN over who owned the rights to *Painted Dreams* and indignantly went to NBC. Within a decade, she had become the "queen of the soaps." Among her other series were *Today's Children, Woman in White, The Brighter Day, As the World Turns* and *The Guiding Light*, the longest-running program in broadcast history (1937–2009). In all, she created or cocreated eighteen radio and TV serials. Although she spent much of her time in New York and California, she considered Chicago her home and died in her house on North Astor Street on December 23, 1973.

By the time Phillips had passed away, Chicago's pioneer broadcasting days were nearly over. One other great sitcom had come out of the city—*Fibber McGee and Molly* (1935)—but soaps and sitcoms had moved to the spacious TV studios of New York and California, although Chicago developed important innovations in TV's early days, such as *Kukla, Fran and Ollie* and *Garroway at Large*, which became the *Today* show. Chicago does, however, have the Museum of Broadcast Communications, founded in 1982, which preserves the city's vivid and varied broadcasting heritage.

32

EUCHARISTIC CONFERENCE BANNER

Roman Catholicism is so intertwined with the history of Chicago that many Chicagoans once identified, not with their neighborhoods, but with their parishes. For examples of the importance of the city's Catholics, who weren't supposed to eat meat on Friday, in old newspapers you can find advertisements for the Ontra Cafeteria announcing the Friday special as "fish or fried shrimps, with tartar sauce," and advertisements for the Stop & Shop Grocery with a section on "Your Friday Fish Dinner." Meanwhile, Kraft Cheese advised, "Instead of Fish on Friday, serve one of the scores of delicious Kraft Elkhorn Cheese dishes." Carl Sandburg called Chicago the "city of the big shoulders." But for a long time, Chicago was identified as "the city of Catholics."

The early French explorers were Catholic, but as a group, Roman Catholics began taking root in Chicago in the 1840s, along with an influx of German and Irish immigrants, the latter fleeing the famine caused by a series of potato crop failures. They were followed by Catholics from Poland, Lithuania, Bohemia, Italy and other European countries, and a great wave of church construction occurred between 1890 and 1930, as ethnic groups competed to erect the most imposing structures, financed largely by the modest contributions of working-class parishioners. At the end of the nineteenth century, the city's archbishops favored a policy of "national" churches, in which each ethnic group could feel at home and masses were given in their own languages. By 1915, 202 national parishes had been established in the city. Under the leadership of American-born George

Eucharistic Conference banner. *Author's collection.*

Mundelein (1872–1939), who, in 1924, became Chicago's first cardinal, the city became a center of Catholic social and pro-labor progressivism, as Mundelein encouraged the establishment of hospitals, daycare centers, youth organizations, adult education classes, orphanages, old-age homes and residences for single mothers. Mundelein considered parochial schools a top priority. In the first three decades of the twentieth century, the number of parochial school students nearly tripled (from 49,638 to 145,116). Like the hospitals and other Catholic social service ventures, these were largely staffed by dedicated nuns.

The zenith of Chicago Catholicism was the Eucharistic Congress of 1926, of which this banner is a memento. The Vatican had been holding Eucharistic Congresses since 1881; this was the first to be hosted in the New World. Pilgrims came from all over the world to be present at what was nicknamed the "Catholic World's Fair." On the first day—June 20— six thousand masses were attended by 1 million people in Chicago's 363 Catholic churches, while three thousand priests heard confessions. The next day, mass was given at Soldier Field in front of 300,000 people. The blare of trumpets rang out, and a women's choir sang the "Mass of the Angels." The *Chicago Tribune* reported that at the stadium's south end, there were

A view of the Eucharistic Congress at Soldier Field. *Library of Congress.*

"hangings of white and yellow—the papal colors…surmounted by staffs carrying gigantic flags of all nations." The congress ended on June 24 with an enormous procession to St. Mary of the Lake Seminary in Mundelein, Illinois (the town had been named after the cardinal in 1924). The souvenir book of the congress proclaimed, "The story of the progress of the Church in Chicago is without parallel and one that fairly staggers the imagination and challenges the credulity."

After World War II, immigrants continued to enlarge the church membership in Chicago. Some were European refugees and others were from the Philippines, but most were from Latin America, especially Mexico. Many parishioners of European heritage moved to the suburbs, and parishes were then being founded outside, not inside, Chicago. By 1990, more Catholics were living in the suburbs than in the city. However, the number of practicing Catholics in both the city and the suburbs waned as society in general experienced increasing secularization. The Archdiocese of Chicago, which covers the city and the surrounding region, reported nearly 2.5 million Catholics in 1970 and about 2.1 million in 2018. Between 1975 and 2019, the number of priests dropped from 1,261 to 746, the number of nuns declined from 6,497 to 1,296, and the number of parishes went from 455 to 336. By the end of the twentieth century, the Chicago archdiocese, once the largest in the United States, ranked third, behind Los Angeles and New York. Under the leadership of Blaise Cupich, who became archbishop in 2014 and cardinal two years later, the archdiocese launched a restructuring program called "Renew My Church." Sadly, for many parishioners, renewal meant consolidation, which involved the closing of some beloved parish churches.

Still, there seems little danger that Chicago will entirely lose its Catholic identity anytime soon. Restaurants and bars have "fish fries" during Lent, and on the day before Ash Wednesday long lines form in front of bakeries selling paczki, the traditional Polish pastry. On Ash Wednesday itself, it's common to see Chicagoans going about their business with ashen crosses on their foreheads, and if St. Patrick's Day occurs on a Friday in Lent, the archdiocese is careful to give dispensation to Catholics who eat corned beef. The fervor of at least some Chicago Catholics can be viewed most dramatically on December 12, the feast day of Our Lady of Guadalupe, when processions travel from several city churches to the Guadalupe shrine in suburban Des Plaines. Some carry statues, some go by bicycle, some go on horseback and some walk barefoot—and the second week of December can get cold in the Windy City.

33

ART DECO ARMCHAIR
BY ABEL FAIDY

When the style known as Art Deco—which is so prized today—was new, it wasn't called "Art Deco." People gave it names like "moderne," "art moderne," "jazz moderne" and, later, "streamlining." Chicago was at the epicenter of the "art moderne" fever. Chicago architects built some of the world's finest Art Deco skyscrapers, and Chicago designers and factories applied the streamlined style to household items—kitchen appliances, furniture, watches, clocks, jewelry, bicycles, radios and more (See "Chicago Bungalow Stained-Glass Window"). When it comes to applying the Art Deco aesthetic to everyday life, it's been said Chicago "made America modern."

The term "Art Deco" became established with the 1968 publication of Bevis Hillier's *Art Deco of the 20s and 30s*. He derived the name from a celebrated 1925 Paris exhibition called *L'Exposition Internationale des Arts Decoratifs et Industriels Moderne* ("arts decoratifs" became "art deco"). It was a vast display of objects, like luxury goods, paintings, furniture and textiles, although some architecture was represented. The motifs that came to exemplify the style could be seen there—geometric patterns, zigzags, lightning bolts, sunbursts, overlapping arches, Aztec and Egyptian designs, abstracted animal forms, stylized bouquets and so on. Chicagoans got to see the new style even while the expo was going on. In June 1925, the John A. Colby furniture store displayed "exact duplicates" of objects shown in France. Shortly afterward, actual objects from Paris were shown in the

Art Deco armchair
by Abel Faidy.
*Chicago History
Museum, ICHi-
031945.*

windows of Marshall Field's Department Store. In the 1930s, Art Deco became less ornate, as designers incorporated the vogue for "streamlining," bringing the influence of machines on contemporary taste. Chicago played a central role in this transition. Its factories churned out a multitude of "moderne" products that were shipped across the country via the city's huge railroad network. Meanwhile, the mail-order catalog giants Sears,

Roebuck and Montgomery Ward, both based in the Windy City, sold Chicago-made Art Deco products, many of which were fashioned from novel materials like aluminum, chrome and Bakelite, which were ideal for the "streamlined" style.

In 1927, Robert Switzer and Harold O. Warner, two young Chicago architects and designers, opened a store called Secession Ltd.; it was the first in Chicago to sell nothing but "moderne" imported furniture, glass, fabrics, pottery and other decorative items. Probably the most dynamic Chicago Art Deco designer was the now nearly forgotten Swiss-born Abel Marius Faidy (1894–1965). After coming to Chicago in 1920, he became a fashionable designer of interiors for offices, showrooms and so on. Faidy designed furniture in a style that has been termed "zigzag modern." For Charles and Ruth Singletary, he produced a stunning fourteen-piece furniture suite; the dining room chairs (one of which is seen here) and the settee evoke the cutbacks of Chicago's Art Deco skyscrapers. For the Hotel Sherman, Faidy created a soda fountain called the Aeroplane Room, which, with its sleek curved lines, "moderne" lettering and streamlining, epitomized Art Deco at its trendiest. Another important Chicago-area Art Deco design firm was W.H. Howell Co., which pioneered tubular metal furniture in the zigzag skyscraper style.

The two Chicago architectural firms most identified with Art Deco were Graham, Anderson, Probst and White (GAPW) and Holabird and Root (known as Holabird and Roche until 1927). Holabird and Root were responsible for what was Chicago's first Art Deco skyscraper, 333 North Michigan Avenue. Its beveled corners give the building what's been called a "ziggurat profile." Other Art Deco buildings from the firm were the Palmolive Building, the Chicago Motor Club, the *Chicago Daily News* Building (now Riverside Plaza), the Buckingham Building, the LaSalle-Wacker Building and, in 1930, their final masterpiece, the soaring Board of Trade Building. Art Deco gems from GAPW include the Merchandise Mart, the Civic Opera House, the Main Post Office, the Shedd Aquarium and the Field Building. Walking into one of their buildings today makes one realize that many of the characteristics that give a structure an Art Deco flair can be seen in the ornamental decoration of the interior. The interior of the Merchandise Mart, for example, is notable for its terrazzo floors, sleek lines, streamlined contours, square fluted piers and stylish murals.

The Great Depression brought skyscraper construction in Chicago to a halt. After GAPW's Field Building was completed in 1934, it was two decades before another major office building was erected in Chicago. And yet, "art moderne" wasn't quite dead in the Windy City, thanks to the great Century of Progress International Exposition of 1933. That illustrious fair, which is the subject of "Century of Progress Exposition Souvenir Box," emphatically verified that Art Deco streamlined modernism was just the thing to epitomize the wonders of advancing technology.

34.

DECCA RECORD OF
"TERRIBLE OPERATION BLUES"

To get a real Chicago experience, the guidebooks assure us, you have to hear some Chicago blues. As *Frommer's Chicago* says, Chicago is "the world capital of the blues," and the music "epitomizes" the city. Could the 1980 movie *The Blues Brothers* really be set anywhere else?

The blues, as a kind of music, has been around for well over a century. The "Chicago blues," however, haven't been around quite as long. Historians of the genre relate that the Chicago blues were born when performers from the Mississippi Delta, like Muddy Waters, Little Walter, Elmore James and Howlin' Wolf, came to the Windy City and began employing electric guitars and harmonicas played through a microphone. This took place after World War II, when many of the bluesmen set up on Maxwell Street, played for the crowds shopping in that well-known street fair of bargains and were discovered by adventurous record labels like Chess, Vee-Jay and J.O.B. The term "Chicago blues" did not become common until the 1970s; before then, the music was usually referred to as "urban blues." But it had such a powerful effect on early rock 'n' roll (in Britain as well as in America) that its influence still resonates like the pick-up of an electric guitar. This is the amplified "Chicago blues" heard in the city's clubs.

Because the word *blue* has been a synonym for *sad* for centuries, it's commonly believed that blues songs are traditionally sad songs. And yet, W.C. Handy, the "father of the blues," once said, "The sorrow songs of the slaves we call Jubilee Melodies. The happy-go-lucky songs of the Southern Negro we call blues." Early blues music was very much dance music. Another

Decca record of "Terrible Operation Blues." *Author's collection.*

assumption is that the blues is a kind of folk music based on "field hollers" or "moans" from antebellum plantations. But the Black men who played the blues in the 1920s thought of themselves as cutting-edge artists who played pop music, not folk music, and they dressed in coats and ties, not overalls. They prided themselves on being able to play not just the blues but just about any hit tune of the day.

Although the "Chicago Blues" emerged after World War II, the blues were heard in Chicago long before then. It's even been reported that Black Texas blues musician Henry Thomas was in Chicago for the 1893 Columbian Exposition. In the 1920s, largely because of recordings, a "blues craze" arose. The leading performers, however, were not guitar-picking Black men, but large-voiced Black women who fronted bands, like Ma Rainey, Bessie

Smith, Lucille Bogan and Mamie Smith, the first Black woman to cut a blues record. All the major "blues queens" performed in Chicago in the 1920s, and their records were big sellers. Reporting on a performance by Mamie Smith, the Black-owned newspaper *Chicago Defender* said, "[She sported] a flock of diamonds that has her lit up like a Polish church on Sunday night." Later in the 1920s, male singer/guitar players began eclipsing the women. Blind Lemon Jefferson, who became the nation's biggest-selling blues artist, made recordings at Marsh Studios in Chicago, as did other bluesmen. Jefferson, however, was not the first Black bluesman to cut a record; that was Papa Charlie Jackson, who, unlike Jefferson, made his home in Chicago. Jackson, the archetype for today's male blues club performers, made sixty-six recordings for Paramount Records. J. Mayo Williams, the Black recording executive who discovered him, said, "You could dance by nearly every song Papa Charlie made." In 1925, Jackson recorded "Maxwell Street Blues"; even then, that thoroughfare was showcasing blues street performers.

The piano player "Georgia Tom," whose name is on the record seen here, was not one of the most prominent blues artists, but he nevertheless became a major figure in the history of Chicago music. His full name was Thomas A. Dorsey. Born in Georgia in 1899, he came to Chicago in 1916, where he first played in after-hours joints known as "buffet flats," private apartments and houses that served bootleg alcohol and sometimes functioned as brothels. Dorsey also became a successful songwriter; his biggest hit was the risqué "It's Tight Like That." Yet, Dorsey, the son of a preacher, continually felt the call of religion, and after suffering a sort of nervous breakdown in 1928, he returned to the church. In 1932, he was appointed choirmaster at the renowned Pilgrim Baptist Church, a position he held for over four decades. But Dorsey didn't renounce his blues background; he adapted it to the requirements of the faith. In doing so, he created the infectious, jubilant choral sound we now know as gospel music. At first, many of the old-time believers were shocked to hear blues-inflected music in church, but today, the gospel sound is practically synonymous with the African American religious experience. It's widely appreciated that Chicago was central to the formation of jazz and blues as foundational American types of music. But Dorsey's long career is a reminder that Chicago also generated a third kind of popular music. Given the way today's pop divas so heavily utilize gospel music techniques, it might even be—at least for now—the most influential type of American music.

35

PROHIBITION LIQUOR PRESCRIPTION

When Prohibition went into effect in the United States on January 17, 1920, Chicago entered the era of bootleg booze, speakeasies, tin lizzies and flappers we now call the "Jazz Age." The manufacture, sale and importation of alcoholic beverages was illegal at the time, but Americans got around the law in many ways. The legislation had exceptions—sacramental wine in churches, cider made on the farm and, as this doctor's prescription shows, physicians and dentists were permitted to prescribe alcohol for "medicinal" purposes. Because of this, pharmacists could stock up on liquor to fill those prescriptions, and they did. In the first six months of Prohibition, fifteen thousand doctors applied for alcohol permits. As for drugstores, Daniel Okrent, in *Last Call: The Rise and Fall of Prohibition*, speculated medicinal alcohol sales were a big reason that Walgreen's, the Chicago-based drugstore chain, grew from twenty stores in 1920 to over five hundred ten years later.

Many other places besides pharmacies sold liquor—although illegally. The *Chicago Tribune* reported Chicagoans were "buying their booze with their shoeshines, with their halibut steaks at the fishmongers, and even at the cobbler's." And the *Chicagoan* magazine wrote, "Groceries, restaurants, cigar stores, laundries, barber shops, all are tempted to dabble a bit." Then there were the speakeasies—clandestine clubs that served illegal drinks. A Chicago anticrime organization estimated that there were twenty thousand speakeasies in the city. Famous Chicago speakeasies included

ORIGINAL
LIQUOR PRESCRIPTION STUB

F111991

9/11/33

DATE PRESCRIBED

John D. Senne

FULL NAME OF PATIENT

ADDRESS 206 S. 4th ave.

NUMBER   STREET

Maywood, Ill.

CITY   STATE

Spt. Fermenti 3 xxxxxx

KIND AND QUANTITY OF LIQUOR PRESCRIBED

3T q 4 hrs. (16 days)

Thos. L. Dwyer   M.D.

SIGN FULL NAME

ADDRESS 232 W. 63rd St.

NUMBER   STREET

Chicago, Ill. 9-17876

CITY   STATE   PERMIT NUMBER

*This stub must be clearly and legibly
written, and must not be detached
from the book.*

85

Prohibition liquor prescription. *Author's collection.*

the Green Mill, the Planet Mars, the Midnight Frolic, the Club Royale, the Rendezvous and the Moulin Rouge. Many of the speakeasies' patrons were women, a sign of a permanent social change. Before, women rarely went to bars, but now, nightlife became "heterosocial," as speakeasies welcomed female patrons. Most speakeasies were not cheap. One of the myths about Prohibition is that the United States was inundated with spirits, but evidence indicates the consumption of alcohol declined by as much as 60 percent. Access to illegal alcohol depended on class. The rich had all the liquor they wanted; the poor, not so much, and some went blind or even died from consuming home brews.

In 1924, a reporter named J.L. Jenkins visited a Chicago automobile show and discovered some of the newest models had hidden spaces "for carrying liquid refreshments." Ironically, the age of Prohibition was probably the golden age of cocktails. An exhibitor at the fifth annual jewelry show in Chicago in 1930 told a reporter, "Cocktail sets are among our staples now. We do a lively trade in women's sterling silver flasks, too. That's one thing prohibition has done—it's helped the jewelry business in that line." Well-off Americans traveled abroad to imbibe—Havana, London and Paris were popular—and so many Yanks went to Canada that the practice was called "alcohol tourism."

Hardware stores sold portable stills for six dollars, and thousands of Chicagoans made liquor at home. Gangsters organized a group of Sicilian families in Little Italy, each operating a still in their apartment. "Bathtub gin" got its name because the bottles they used were jugs or carboys; they were too tall to fit in the sink, so they required the use of bathtub faucets to top them off with water. Many police officers were on a mobster's payroll. An estimated 60 percent of the police force was in the liquor business, and at one station, the policemen lined up at the end of the month for their payoffs ($10 to $125 each). As the *Tribune* wrote, "A man in police uniform has a good many opportunities to operate as a bootlegger, with his uniform as protection."

Books on mixing drinks continued to be published. Examples include *Here's How!* by "Judge Jr." (1927), *Giggle Water* (1928), *Cheerio!* (1928) and *The Drinks of Yesteryear: A Mixology* (1930). There's a lot of misinformation about Jazz Age cocktails, but by studying the manuals, it's possible to identify seven that were actually consumed in the Windy City—the Garnet, Ticonderoga, Years of Grace, Woman of Fashion, Armour, Chicago, and Poets and Their Art. Here are recipes for the last three:

Armour
(Charlie Roe and Jim Schwenk, *The Home Bartender's Guide and Song Book*, 1930)

Three dashes of orange bitters
Half a jigger of sherry
Half a jigger of Italian Vermouth (red)

Shake with ice. Strain into a cocktail glass and add a piece of orange peel.

▼▼▼▼▼▼▼▼

Chicago
(John Drury, *Dining in Chicago*, 1931)

One or two dashes of Angostura Bitters
Three dashes of Curaçao
Half a gill of brandy
Champagne

A U.S. gill is four ounces. Fill the mixing glass half full of broken ice, add the bitters, Curaçao and brandy. "Stir well, strain into cocktail glass; add an olive or cherry, squeeze a lemon peel and drop it into the glass, and pour a little Champagne on top. Before straining the mixture into the cocktail glass, moisten the outside borders of the glass with lemon juice and dip into pulverized sugar."

▼▼▼▼▼▼▼▼

Poets and Their Art—as consumed by Chicago poet Harriet Monroe
(Sterling North and Carl Kroch, *So Red the Nose, or Breath in the Afternoon*, 1935)

One-part gin
One-part canned grapefruit juice

"Ice and serve." That's it. No wonder Monroe was a champion of modern minimalism in the arts.

36.

GUNS FROM THE ST. VALENTINE'S DAY MASSACRE

I t's amazing to realize that the guns used in the infamous St. Valentine's Day Massacre still exist. But they do, and they're in the possession of the Berrien County Sheriff's Department in St. Joseph, Michigan.

The St. Valentine's Day Massacre took place on February 14, 1929, inside a garage on North Clark Street in Chicago. Four hitmen, two dressed as police officers, lined up seven members of the Bugs Moran gang and gunned them all down. Chicago crime boss Al Capone was immediately suspected, but he was conveniently in Florida at the time. In *Al Capone's Beer Wars: A Complete History of Organized Crime in Chicago During Prohibition*, historian John J. Binder, after a painstaking analysis, argued that, although Capone was probably behind the murders, the actual crime was most likely plotted by an independent crew called the West Side Circus Café Gang, which might have brought in outsiders to do the actual shooting.

Ten months later, a police officer in St. Joseph, Michigan, pulled over an intoxicated driver in what should have been a routine traffic stop, but the driver fatally shot the officer and drove away. He later wrecked his car and fled on foot. The retrieved car enabled the police to locate the driver's bungalow, and there, they found an arsenal of weapons, including two Thompson submachine guns. In Chicago, ballistics expert Calvin Goddard, using spent cartridges from the murder scene, determined that the submachine guns had been used in the massacre.

It's no wonder that the authorities suspected Capone. Alphonse Capone (1899–1947) was not just the most famous gangster in the Windy City, he

Guns from the St. Valentine's Day Massacre. *Photograph courtesy of Chriss Lyon, the author of* A Killing in Capone's Playground: The True Story of the Hunt for the Most Dangerous Man Alive.

was probably the most famous American in the world. So many stories have been told about him that it's hard to separate fact from legend. For example, some people imagine him as short, but a police record that is now in the Smithsonian Institution records "Big Al" as being six feet and one-half inch tall. English was his first language, he spoke without the tough guy "dese and dose" of filmdom and many were impressed by his good manners. Capone used to say, "I'm no Italian, I was born in Brooklyn," and only about 60 percent of his gang members were Italian. Also, Capone had almost nothing to do with the Mafia—the Mafia was Sicilian, and his family was Neapolitan. Another misconception is he was the boss of all Chicago. About a dozen gangs fought over the city's turf, and although Capone made alliances with some, others remained rivals. Capone traveled surrounded by bodyguards and once said, "I haven't had any peace of mind in years. Every minute, I'm in danger of death."

Probably the biggest myth about Capone was that he was essentially harmless and did a lot of good. For example, one woman said at the time, "You can say what you want about Al Capone. If people were desperate and needed help, he was there to help them." Prohibition was widely viewed as a foolish law, and flouting it was generally more admired than condemned. Besides liquor, Capone made money from gambling, but that was usually considered a victimless crime. And as for the murders he ordered, the victims were themselves killers and not to be mourned. Capone famously said, "I've been spending the best years of my life as a public benefactor.... My booze has been good and my games on the square." Capone, however, conveniently neglected to mention that his operation included dozens of brothels in which women were terrorized and sold off like slaves. Also, he was involved with narcotics and labor racketeering. Once in control of a labor union, Capone could pilfer the pension funds and extort bribes from employers for calling off a strike. Eventually, he controlled the plumbers, sanitation workers, street cleaners, steamfitters, construction workers and several transportation unions. Muscling in on legitimate businesses was also lucrative. In 1929, the Employees' Association of Chicago counted ninety-one businesses that had been infiltrated by the mob, which forced these businesses to increase prices, after which they skimmed off the extra cash. It was a kind of racketeering tax that the Chicago Crime Commission estimated cost consumers $200 million a year. Wringing that much money out of working folk hardly qualifies as a public benefit.

In the end, it was not a rival gangster who brought down Capone, but a team of accountants. The authorities were almost embarrassed that they couldn't pin a murder rap on him and had to convict him on tax evasion, but on November 24, 1931, he was sentenced to eleven years in federal prison, fined $50,000 and charged $7,692 for court costs. He spent most of his prison term in Alcatraz until he was released in November 1939. By then, his mind was nearly gone due to the effects of syphilis, and he died in Florida on January 25, 1947.

As for the submachine guns found in Michigan, the fugitive who had stored them in his house was identified as Chicago mobster Fred "Killer" Burke. The subject of a national manhunt, Burke was eventually captured, tried and sent to prison in Michigan. He never confessed to participating in the massacre, nor did he reveal how he got the guns. Although he understandably remains a prime suspect, his participation is still unproven, and the most notorious murder in Chicago's gangland history remains unsolved.

37.

CENTURY OF PROGRESS EXPOSITION SOUVENIR BOX

Chicagoans were so proud of the 1933 Century of Progress Exposition that they made it the fourth star on the city flag. When the fair was being planned in the late 1920s, it was intended to be a centennial commemoration of Chicago's incorporation as a town in 1833. The theme was "progress," which was appropriate because, at the time, technology was unveiling wonders nearly every day—from airships in the skies to radios in the parlor. But while celebrating progress, the organizers were blindsided by something unforeseen—the Great Depression. So, by the time the exposition opened in May 1933, the theme of recovery had been added—recovery through science. "You probably have heard over the radio that 'all the world is waiting for the sunrise,'" one fair official said. "A Century of Progress may be the business sunrise that the world is waiting for, and it will be a demonstration of the splendid strength and vitality of the city of Chicago."

The exposition stretched along the shore of Lake Michigan, from the Adler Planetarium south to Thirty-Ninth Street. The fashionable Art Deco style of streamlined modernism formed the overall architectural look, and the buildings were painted with a flamboyant multihued palette, giving the exposition the nickname "Rainbow City" (in contrast to the "White City" of 1893). Colored lighting provided by miles of gas-filled tubes added to the polychrome riot.

The Travel and Transport Building, which is pictured on this souvenir box, was designed by Edward H. Bennett, John Holabird and Hubert

Century of Progress Exposition souvenir box. *Author's collection.*

Burnham, and it was one of the first buildings to be constructed for the exposition. It consisted of a domed roof that was attached by long cables to twelve surrounding towers. As the official guidebook explained, "For the first time in architectural history, a dome has been constructed on the principle of a suspension bridge." Because there were no interior columns, the exhibit space was entirely unobstructed. Hanging from the ceiling high above was a Boeing 247 passenger plane, while other exhibits comprised an old stagecoach "scarred by bullets and Indian arrows"; the *Pioneer*, the first locomotive to run out of Chicago (See "Railroad Fair Pennant"); a complete oil well derrick; and a glass automobile. Also featured was a huge illuminated map that showed "a lighted network of airways serving forty-four states."

The technological wonders of the fair were many. At its center was the Hall of Science, a modernist edifice capped by a 175-foot-tall bell tower; among its exhibits were a geological time clock, a life-sized transparent man and a model of a molecule of salt. The General Electric Pavilion featured popcorn bursting in a microwave, and Westinghouse presented an X-ray machine and a robot named Willie that not only talked but smoked. In the AT&T Building, visitors could place a long-distance phone call to any of the fifty-four cities displayed on a huge electric map. Perhaps the most revelatory exhibit displayed a television; it was surprisingly put on by the Hudson-Essex Motor Company. The "supreme thrill of the fair" was the Sky Ride, in which passengers rode in double-decker "rocket cars" on cables 219 feet above the lagoon.

Despite all the futuristic marvels, however, what many fairgoers remembered best was a woman with no clothes on—a formerly unemployed actress and dancer named Sally Rand, who appeared in a show called *Streets of Paris*. There, she did her titillating fan dance, in which she teasingly concealed her body behind moving ostrich feathers (until the end, when she lowered them).

The Century of Progress Exposition ran for two seasons (1933–1934). The directors reported an attendance of 50 million, and even though there was a depression, it made money. It was estimated that out-of-town visitors pumped $700,000,000 into Chicago's economy. As the expo closed its gates, fair president Rufus C. Dawes commented, "It will live in our memories. Were we to live a thousand years, we would never forget it, for it lifted up our spirits, restored our souls, and brought us hope. This exposition spoke to a world in distress, and it spoke with the authentic voice of Chicago, asserting pride and announcing faith."

The Sky Ride at the Century of Progress Exposition. *Author's collection.*

38

WORLD WAR II RATION BOOK

I t was a Chicagoan—Studs Terkel—who called World War II "the good war." Now that the number of people who remember that conflict is dwindling, the rest of us tend to idealize it as a time when Americans were united, filled with purpose and confident that destroying Nazi Germany was a worthy crusade. But in the title of his *"The Good War": An Oral History of World War II*, Terkel put "The Good War" in quotation marks because, as he explained, coupling the adjective *good* to the noun *war* was "so incongruous." Terkel's history appeared just nine years after the Vietnam War ended, and compared to that divisive, futile struggle, World War II didn't look so bad.

But when the war began, Chicagoans didn't find it good—they found it terrifying. The Japanese were sweeping through the southwest Pacific, and German submarines were sinking ships right off the Atlantic coast. The U.S. surgeon general insisted the enemy was planning bacteriological warfare, while Chicago mayor Edward Kelly warned, "Don't let anyone tell you that you are too far away from the battle for aerial attack. Chicago is a danger zone." Volunteer air raid wardens scrutinized the skies, and Chicagoans staged "blackouts," turning out all of their lights at night to foil potential enemy bombardiers. Fears that America could lose the war were common. In September 1942, Ralph A. Bard, assistant secretary of the navy, put it bluntly when he said, "We are still losing this war, period. And should damn well understand it, period." Some three million men entered the military in the first year of the war, and the dread that loved ones would not return was real. Insomnia was rampant.

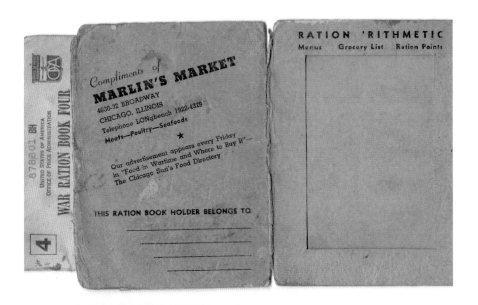

World War II ration book. *Author's collection.*

This ration book speaks of another strain: shortages of every kind. Its tiny tear-off tickets permitted consumers to purchase limited quantities of rationed foodstuffs. As recounted in *We've Got a Job to Do: Chicagoans and World War II* by Perry Duis and Scott LaFrance, the first item to be rationed was sugar (one pound every two weeks), followed by meat, fats, cheese, butter, coffee and canned fruits and vegetables. Hoarding was widespread, and although "victory gardens" were numerous, they never provided more than a fraction of what was needed. New cars disappeared as automobile factories turned to building tanks and planes. Used cars soared in value, but even those who could get one found that tires and gasoline were strictly rationed. Chicagoans took part in scrap drives as they were urged to search for wastepaper, old rubber, aluminum cookware, rags and metal in nearly any form, including paper clips and shoe nails. Collecting cooking grease and fat was imperative, and used fat containers were placed on street corners. Because factories were booming, the horrendous unemployment rates of the Great Depression were gone, and Chicagoans had more money than they had seen in years, but there was little to buy.

Chicago played a crucial role in the production of war materials. Some examples of the Chicago industries that were refitted for war included

Vaughn Manufacturing (bomb fuses), the Pressed Steel Car Company (armored vehicles), Western Electric (radar), Goss Printing (navy guns) and Radio Flyer (gasoline cans). Chicago's food-processing firms turned out enormous amounts of military rations. In addition to existing enterprises, nearly three hundred new factories were built—the gigantic new Dodge-Chicago factory, for example, assembled the C-47 transport plane. In all, Chicago received $9.2 billion in defense contracts during the war.

One of the most enduring images of World War II was "Rosie the Riveter," that formidable female factory hand who freed up a male worker for the military. And Chicago had a lot of Rosies—although some jobs, such as those in steel mills, remained mostly male. Many women worked in defense plants—at the Elwood Arsenal, for example, they loaded TNT into bombs—but women replaced men in many other positions, such as those of garbage collectors, truck drivers, traffic cops, railroad workers, elevator operators, bank clerks and office personnel of all types. By 1944, according to Duis and LaFrance, 43 percent (300,000) of the women in Chicagoland were in the workforce. Chicagoland also played a large role in military training; one-third of all U.S. Navy personnel spent some time at the Great Lakes Naval Training Center, while army soldiers trained at Fort Sheridan, and 10,000 pilots trained at Glenview Naval Air Station. Chicago offered four servicemen's centers, and members of the military considered the Windy City "the best GI town in America." Finally, it was at the University of Chicago that physicist Enrico Fermi led the project that ultimately resulted in the development of the atomic bomb.

One last source of anxiety was that no one knew how long the war would last. Some estimated that it would last for ten years. But it did end—in Europe on May 8, 1945 and in Asia on August 14, 1945. The headline in the *Chicago Tribune* on August 15 was "Joyous Bedlam Loosed in City." Thousands of celebrants jammed the Loop. "They were noisy. They represented all ages and all classes. Elderly men and women were as numerous as bobby soxers." Mayor Kelly called it "a victory for the decent people of the world against maniac gangsters." And a *Tribune* editorial said, "It is time, and more than time, that all Americans hold high their heads with pride."

39

RAILROAD FAIR PENNANT

For some time, Chicago has been known as "the railroad capital of America." The organizers of the 1948 Railroad Fair, of which this pennant was a popular souvenir, went further, calling Chicago "the greatest transportation center in all creation."

Chicago's geographic position has made it a travel hub from the era of Native trails to the eras of canals, railroads and air travel. The city's first railroad, the Galena and Chicago Union Railway, began operating in 1848, along with Chicago's first steam locomotive, the *Pioneer*. Competing railroads proliferated in Chicago, and within a decade, some three thousand miles of track on seventeen railroads radiated from the Windy City, and one hundred trains were entering and departing from the city daily. A vital factor in Chicago's railroad supremacy was that no railroad ran *through* the city; trains only began and ended there, which meant through passengers had to change trains. This sometimes involved an overnight stay. Similarly, for grain, meat, coal and other products, Chicago was the end of the line. At first, Chicago's railroads went west and south, the idea being that products shipped to Chicago by rail would then be transferred to Great Lakes freighters. But railroads from the East drew ever closer until Chicago was finally linked to the East Coast in 1853. Three years later, the *Chicago Tribune*, in a piece called "Points of the Triangle," compared Chicago to St. Louis and Cincinnati, its rival cities of the West, and concluded that its railroad network would bring Chicago preeminence: "From the fact that the region of which it is the trading center is constantly increasing, and that, with marvelous rapidity,

Railroad Fair pennant. *Author's collection.*

this growth of Chicago must keep pace. All things considered, its progress is more wonderful than that of any city in the Union, and its future is likely to be as astonishing as its past."

The railroads brought what was needed to support major industries, like the stockyards, steel and the warehousing of agricultural products, but Chicago, in turn, serviced the railroads by fabricating track and freight cars (both made of Chicago steel) and housing repair shops. The city's manufacturers also turned out lanterns, wheels and switches. The most prominent rail car maker was the huge Pullman Company, the builder of sleeping cars (see "Pullman Porter Cap"), but Chicago also manufactured thousands of refrigerator cars, the innovation of stockyard giant Gustavus Swift, as well as a vast number of tank cars.

It's hard to visualize today because nearly all of it is gone, but in the 1930s, downtown Chicago was crammed with railroad terminals and warehouses. Block after block of warehouses spread north of the river, west of LaSalle Street and south of Roosevelt Road. Thirty-six railroads fed into Chicago's six major downtown passenger stations—Central, Dearborn, La Salle Street, Grand Central, Union and the C&NW Passenger Terminal. Designed to impress, their cavernous interiors, high ceilings and bell towers were reminiscent of cathedrals. The number of stations could be confusing, especially when travelers had to transfer from one to another. The *Daily News Almanac and Year-Book for 1926* estimated that 264,000 travelers passed through the stations every day (about 83,000 were commuters). It was the golden age of rail travel, as competition obliged the lines to offer superior service and faster speeds—hence the streamlined trains of the 1930s (and

Chicago was *the* place to board them). For example, the main courses on the dining car dinner menu of the Twentieth Century Limited, which ran between Chicago and New York, included broiled lake trout, lobster newburg, prime rib and "broiled Shrewsbury squab."

The Railroad Fair of 1948–1949 was Chicago's self-congratulatory centennial celebration of its first railroad. Thirty-nine railroads were represented at the fairgrounds, which stretched along the lakefront from Twenty-First Street to Thirty-First Street. Among the attractions were a narrow-gauge train ride called "Deadwood Central," a Florida garden, a working replica of the Old Faithful Geyser, a corral for western shows, a large miniature railroad and an adobe village that housed 150 members of several western Native tribes who performed ceremonial dances. The high point of the fair was the *Wheels a-Rolling* pageant, which reenacted America's transportation history through fourteen tableaux, beginning with "The Voyageurs, 1673" and continuing through such spectacles as "The Iron Horse, 1829–36," "Chicago, 1848," "The Golden Spike,

The "Wheels a-Rolling" Pageant at the Chicago Railroad Fair. *Wikimedia Commons.*

1869," "The Gay Nineties" and "Pioneer Zephyr, 1934." Viewers watched as some half-dozen antique locomotives, including the *Pioneer*, steamed down the tracks.

The Railroad Fair had a nostalgic tone; it was obvious that the era of cross-country railroad passenger travel was ending, but railroads hardly became obsolete. Today, the U.S. rail network has some 140,000 miles of track, carries one-third of U.S. exports and delivers 5 million tons of freight and over 80,000 passengers every day. Many view shipping by rail as preferable to trucking. According to the Association of American Railroads, moving freight by rail is four times more fuel efficient than moving freight on the highway, which makes rail shipping better for the environment. Trains also don't get stuck in traffic, and they can carry extremely large loads. Chicago was, and remains, "the Rome of the railroads," as it was called in the nineteenth century. It's an Amtrak hub, and even today, freight cars that cross the country are squeezed into Chicagoland to be sorted and placed on other lines to continue their trips. According to the *Encyclopedia of Chicago*, "More lines radiate in more directions from Chicago than from any other city."

40

PIZZERIA UNO MATCHBOOK

Frommer's Chicago says, "Going out for deep-dish pizza is pretty much a requirement for any family visiting Chicago." The Windy City has a well-deserved reputation for being a pizza center. Food reporter Steve Dolinsky's survey of the Chicago's pizza scene is titled *Pizza City, USA: 101 Reasons Why Chicago is America's Greatest Pizza Town.*

The standard history of Chicago's love affair with the crusty pie from Naples begins with deep-dish pizza. It was developed at the dining establishment advertised on this matchbook—Pizzeria Uno. When it opened in 1943, it was known as Pizzeria Riccardo or just the Pizzeria, but when its sister restaurant, Pizzeria Due, opened in 1955, the original spot became Pizzeria Uno.

Phil Vettel, a food critic for the *Chicago Tribune*, once said, "Chicago-style pizza may owe its existence to a bad enchilada." A Chicago businessman named Ike Sewell partnered with Italian-born Ric Riccardo (originally Richard Novaretti), to purchase a bar, and they turned it into a restaurant. At first, they planned on serving Mexican food, but after visiting a Mexican restaurant to learn more about the cuisine, Riccardo got sick—Mexican was out. The back-up plan was pizza, which Americans were learning about from returning GIs who had discovered it in Italy. Sewell, however, wanted something more substantial than the thin pies consumed in Naples, so he came up with the thick, hefty pie that is now identified with the Windy City. Who developed the recipe is up for debate; although, it almost certainly was not Sewell, who wasn't a chef. Many historians credit Riccardo, although

**29 EAST OHIO ST.
CHICAGO, ILLINOIS
(312) 321-1000**

DIAMOND MATCH DIV. ◆ CHICAGO, ILLINOIS

CHICAGO, ILLINOIS
619 N. WABASH
PIZZERIA DUE
(312) 943-2400

PIZZERIA UNO

"IKE SEWELL'S ORIGINAL CHICAGO PIZZA"

CLOSE COVER ● STRIKE MATCH ON BACK

Pizzeria Uno matchbook. *Author's collection.*

some suggest that one of two other Uno employees might have done it (or at least contributed): bartender Adolpho "Rudy" Malnati Sr. or cook Alice Mae Redmond, an African American woman who later became a partner and pizza maker at Gino's East, a deep-dish outlet that opened in 1966. Other people with Pizzeria Uno connections later started their own deep-dish places. Rudy Malnati's son, Lou, opened a pizzeria in 1971, and there are now several dozen Lou Malnati's restaurants in Chicagoland. Another offshoot was Pizano's (1991), which was created by Rudy Malnati Jr., Lou Malnati's half-brother.

Although Pizzeria Uno began the deep-dish tradition, Chicago's Italian immigrants were eating pizza long before Ike Sewell. According to *The Chicago Food Encyclopedia*, Chicago's first pizzeria was Granato's (later named Pizzeria Napolitana). Most sources state it opened in the early 1930s, but a vintage postcard shows an outdoor sign reading "Established Since 1924." Granato's, which closed in 1961, was in Chicago's Italian enclave along Taylor Street and was seemingly unknown to people outside the neighborhood. In 1931, a reporter named John Drury published a restaurant guide called *Dining in Chicago*, and although he reviewed many Italian eateries and mentioned spaghetti dozens of times, he did not refer to pizza once. In August 1941, the *Chicago Tribune* announced an upcoming Italian grape festival and said that the booths would be serving "wines, beer, clams, Italian barbecued sausage, and pizza," perhaps the first mention of the pie in the Chicago press. A year later, Mary Meade, a reporter for the same newspaper, advised readers to try Pizzeria Napolitana (Granato's), and it's obvious that she didn't expect them to know what pizza was. "Pizza is a wonderful yeast dough 'pie,' with tomatoes and cheese and seasonings baked upon it. You eat it in pie shaped wedges and is it good!" Other early pizzerias included Jim & Pete's (1941), Vito & Nick's (1946), Father and Son (1947), Home Run Inn (1947), Italian Fiesta Pizzeria (1947), Candlelite (1950), Marie's (1950) and Pat's Pizza (1950). Pizza really took off in Chicago in the early 1950s. According to the *Tribune* in 1953, "Sixteen short years ago, there wasn't a pizzeria in the Chicago classified telephone directory. Today, there are more than a hundred, and the neon signs shout 'Pizza' all over town."

These over one hundred pizzerias were not all serving deep-dish pizza. Although deep-dish has become one of Chicago's most representative food items, the city's pizza reputation doesn't depend on its deep-dish but on its variety. Many—maybe most—Chicago pizza mavens don't even like deep-dish that much. In *Pizza City, USA*, Dolinsky counted no fewer than ten types of pie in Chicago: tavern-style, thin, New York-style, artisan, Neapolitan, deep-dish, stuffed, Sicilian, Roman and Detroit-style. Of these, tavern style (also known as "Chicago-style thin") is the most prevalent and popular. Tavern-style, it's said, is so called because bar owners wanted a pie with small pieces so patrons could hold a portion in one hand and drink a beer with the other. Tavern style is cut in a grid, not wheel spokes as in New York. This means the inner pieces have no crust (which some diners like). Toppings? That's another thing that makes Chicago pizza different. Just about anywhere in the United States, pizzeria surveys report pepperoni is clearly the favorite. However, in the Windy City, for some reason, it's sausage by far. A curious tourist who wants to try tavern-style at its finest will have to venture outside the Loop, which is a good idea anyway. And so as to blend in, the visitor should make sure to order "saah-sage."

41.

MIES VAN DER ROHE APARTMENTS PLAYING CARDS

Tourists who visit Chicago for more than a few days are bound to hear the name Mies van de Rohe (1886–1969), especially if they go on an architecture tour. Although the celebrated architect was born in Germany and didn't come to Chicago until he was fifty-two, his impact on the city was indelible.

Mies (his birth name was Maria Ludwig Michael Mies, which he changed to Ludwig Mies van der Rohe, but he was always called just "Mies") never formally studied architecture. He learned from his father, a master mason, attended trade school in his native Aachen and then became a draftsman in a factory that made ceiling decorations. In 1905, he went to Berlin, attended arts and crafts schools and fine arts schools and went to work first for the progressive architect Bruno Paul. He later worked for the famed modernist Peter Behrens. Mies's work during the 1920s marked him as an up-and-coming theoretician and designer, a reputation sealed by his German Pavilion for the 1929 International Exposition in Barcelona. By 1930, he was the director of the legendary Bauhaus, a kind of modernist art school/think tank whose staff, at one time or another, boasted some of the biggest names in modern art—Walter Gropius, Paul Klee, Wassily Kandinsky, Josef Albers and László Moholy-Nagy. In Mies's youth, the European avant-garde style was adopting a revolutionary aesthetic that included abstract and nonobjective art, twelve-tone music, antinarrative poetry and nonrepresentational sculpture and stage design. A component of the ideology was the idea that figurative art or decorated architecture

Mies van der Rohe Apartments playing cards. *Author's collection.*

obscured the real meaning, the essence, of things, making it necessary to strip away the superficial and favor a kind of mystical minimalism. As early as 1910, architect Adolf Loos proclaimed, "Ornament is a crime." In architecture, this creed led to the "International Style," characterized most famously by the steel-and-glass skyscrapers that Mies dubbed "skin-and-bones" architecture. The style's hallmarks were planar forms, pure colors, clean lines, and the unadorned expression of the "innate" qualities of industrial materials. As Mies famously expressed it, "Less is more."

The Nazis closed the Bauhaus in 1933. Mies remained in Germany, but commissions were scarce, and he left in 1937. In a stroke of fortunate timing, the Illinois Institute of Technology (IIT) was seeking someone to head its architecture school. Chicago architect John Holabird recommended Mies, telling the school president, Henry Heald, "He is so much better than any of the people you could get to head a school of architecture. Why not take a chance?" Heald took quite a chance, giving Mies an almost unheard-of opportunity: to design a completely new twenty-building campus covering eight city blocks. Today, IIT is in the National Register of Historic Places and is a regular stop for tour groups. Mies (and many others) considered S.R. Crown Hall, which houses the school's College of Architecture, to be his most perfect building. Elsewhere in Chicago, Mies was given opportunities he never had in Europe: the Promontory Apartments (1948), the 860–880 Lake Shore Apartments (1951), the Commonwealth Promenade Apartments (1956), the 2400 North Lakeview Condos (1963), the Chicago Federal Center (1964) and One IBM Plaza (1970). Herbert S. Greenwald and Samuel N. Katzin, the developers of the Esplanade Apartment Buildings (1956), evidently thought it would help sales to give away these promotional playing cards, an advertising practice that was common when card playing was a major social activity. Also known as 900/910 Lake Shore Drive, these high-rises have been acclaimed for Mies's perfection of the "curtain wall," which sheathes them in a practically uninterrupted surface of glass.

Mies's followers were legion, and soon American cities were being filled with "glass boxes." The backlash was fast in coming. Mies wasn't even dead when architect Robert Venturi, a pioneer of "postmodernism," said, "Less is a bore," and the irreverent *From Bauhaus to Our House* (1981) by the social critic Tom Wolfe skewered the posturings of the academics who worshipped at the Miesian shrine. Wolfe viewed American intellectuals as victims of a "colonial complex," in which they assumed the European avant-garde was superior to anything on the parochial American artistic scene. Other cultural historians have made a similar argument, pointing out that the arts in America were doing just fine before the arrival of European émigrés who were fleeing Nazism and World War II (Aaron Copland in music, Edward Hopper in painting, Frank Lloyd Wright in architecture).

And then, as it happens in cultural history, the pendulum swung back. Critics came to realize Mies's reputation had been sullied by the dreary imitations of followers who lacked his sensitivity and discrimination. Even Venturi came to regret his "less is a bore" quip. Paul Goldberger, an architecture critic of the *New York Times*, observed that talented modern architects like Mies were good at designing individual buildings but not so good at constructing cities. One glass box can be inspiring, but a line of them is deadening (exhibit A: Sixth Avenue in Manhattan). Chicago is fortunate. The city doesn't have long rows of mind-numbing glass boxes, but it does have elegant and prominent single buildings by Mies, its adopted son.

42.

NELSON ALGREN'S TYPEWRITER

Later in his life, Chicago writer Nelson Algren (1909–1981) held an apartment sale at his residence on Evergreen Street before moving to the East Coast. Algren's friend Art Shay retrieved Algren's typewriter, on which Algren had written *The Man with the Golden Arm*, from a repair shop. The typewriter ended up in the possession of a friend of Shay, who later donated it to the Nelson Algren Museum of Miller Beach in Gary, Indiana, where Algren had a beach cabin. It is a rare and invaluable memento, not only of a writer whose reputation has risen in recent years, but also of Chicago's distinguished literary history.

The first stirrings of literary life in Chicago began when it was still a rough frontier town (with a population of just four thousand). Horatio Cooke's *Gleanings of Thought* (1843) was the first volume of poetry published in Chicago; a few works of frontier fiction appeared in the 1850s, followed in 1856 by *Wau-bun, the "Early Day" in the North-West*, a novel/memoir by Juliette Augusta Magill Kinzie, the daughter-in-law of pioneer John Kinzie (see "Mark Beaubien's Fiddle"). *Barriers Burned Away* (1872) by the immensely popular E.P. Roe, introduced what was to become a common theme—the arrival in the city of a young person who must overcome its obstacles and temptations. Chicago began to get national attention in the 1890s, when the city's writers developed the country's first urban literature. *The Cliff-Dwellers* (1893) and *With the Procession* (1895) by Henry Blake Fuller (1857–1929) won praise from the likes of William Dean Howells and H.L. Mencken for their critiques of city life. George Ade (1866–1944) proved to be a master of urban

Nelson Algren's typewriter. *Nelson Algren Museum of Miller Beach.*

lingo in works like *Artie* (1896), *Pink Marsh* (1897) and, especially, *Fables in Slang* (1899). And Finley Peter Dunne (1867–1936) gave American literature one of its most unforgettable characters—the Irish American bartender/philosopher Mr. Dooley, who gave us such maxims as "politics ain't beanbag" and "thrust ivrybody—but cut th' ca-ards." In 1917, Mencken uttered his legendary appraisal of the Windy City's writers: "I give you Chicago. It is not London-and-Harvard. It is not Paris-and-buttermilk. It is American in every chitling and sparerib, and it is alive from snout to tail."

Many writers followed the trail blazed by Fuller, Ade and Dunne. Frank Norris (1870–1902) proved to be a master of naturalism in *McTeague* and his unfinished trilogy *The Epic of Wheat* (see "Chicago Board of Trade Necktie"), while *The Jungle*, the exposé of Chicago's meatpacking industry by Upton Sinclair (1878–1968), was a sensation. Theodore Dreiser (1871–1945) wrote some of the most admired novels of the twentieth century, such as *The Financier* and *The Titan*, which were based on the Chicago traction mogul Charles T. Yerkes (See "Alderman Michael 'Hinky Dink' Kenna's Badge"). If for nothing else, Chicago owes a debt to poet Carl Sandburg (1878–1967) for labeling the city the "hog butcher for the world," the "stacker of wheat" and, most enduringly, the "city of the big shoulders." The Studs Lonigan trilogy by James T. Farrell (1904–1979) described the milieu of the working-class South Side Irish, while Richard Wright (1908–1960) explored the stressful conditions of the South Side's African American community, which was also the focus of the poetry of Gwendolyn Brooks (1917–2000) and *A Raisin in the Sun*, the groundbreaking play by Lorraine Hansberry (1930–1965). In novelist Saul Bellow (1915–2005), Chicago found its only Nobel Prize–winning author (unless you count Ernest Hemingway of Oak Park, who didn't much identify with the city). Later, Chicago writers who won national reputations included playwright David Mamet, the author of *Glengarry Glen Ross* and *American Buffalo*; Scott Turow, a specialist in legal thrillers; poet, novelist and short story writer Stuart Dybek; Sara Paretsky, the creator of the female private eye V.I. Warshawski; and Mexican American writer Sandra Cisneros, the author of *The House on Mango Street*.

This brings us back to the writer who left his typewriter behind. (Many previous writers who had gotten their start in Chicago also went east. First, Dunne and Ade; then Dreiser, Hamlin Garland, Edna Ferber, Sherwood Anderson, Ben Hecht, Edgar Lee Masters, Ring Lardner and Farrell.) The writings of Chicago's authors are often described as "hard-boiled" or "gritty" in their depictions of the city's rough edges. Nowhere is this truer than in Algren's novels, with their unsparing depictions of alcoholics, drug addicts, prostitutes, corrupt politicians, flophouse residents and various wannabes whose dreams will never find fulfillment. Algren's fame peaked with the 1955 film adaption of *The Man with the Golden Arm*, which starred Frank Sinatra and which Algren hated, and then it declined. In recent years, however, his reputation has grown, partly because of two biographies— *Algren: A Life* by Mary Wisniewski and *Never a Lovely So Real: The Life and Work of Nelson Algren* by Colin Asher. In a review of the latter in the *New York Review of Books*, Andrew O'Hagan called Algren "Chicago's answer to Dostoevsky" and said, "His time has arrived." The title of Asher's book also serves as a reminder that Algren penned, in his *Chicago: A City on the Make*, a capsule description of Algren's hometown that was worthy of standing beside Sandburg's "city of the big shoulders": "Like loving a woman with a broken nose, you may well find lovelier lovelies. But never a lovely so real."

43

COOK COUNTY HOSPITAL RESEARCH POSTCARD

Chicago is thought of as a terrific sports town, a great city for restaurants, a transportation hub, a high-tech magnet and a major educational center, but people sometimes overlook Chicago's standing as one of the world's finest medical centers. One-fifth of all the doctors in the United States have received all or part of their training in the Windy City, and the Illinois Medical District, located west of Ashland Avenue, is the first and largest urban medical district in the country.

Chicago's first official hospital opened in 1843—although it wasn't a hospital as we think of one today. It was a place to isolate victims of the city's frequent epidemics. Other early Chicago hospitals focused on caring for the poor, the incapacitated and the insane. The city's first medical school, Rush Medical College, was chartered on March 2, 1837, just two days before the city of Chicago was incorporated. Ten years later, physicians from Rush opened Chicago's first general hospital. Being found to be too small, it was replaced in 1852 by the larger Mercy Hospital, so called because it was staffed by the Sisters of Mercy, a Roman Catholic order of nuns. Among the hospitals that followed were the Illinois Charitable Eye and Ear Infirmary (1858), St. Luke's (1865), Passavant (1865), Michael Reese (1866), Children's Memorial (1882), Wesley Memorial (1888) and Chicago Baptist (1891). As historian Thomas Bonner wrote in *Medicine in Chicago, 1850–1950*, by 1893, Chicago "could boast four regular medical schools, two post-graduate institutions, a dozen medical societies, numerous

Cook County Hospital research postcard. *Author's collection.*

hospitals and clinics, ten medical journals, and more than twelve hundred regular practitioners of medicine."

One of those more than 1,200 practitioners was Daniel Hale Williams, one of the most fascinating figures in Chicago medical history. He was an African American who was born in Pennsylvania in 1856 to a middle-class family. His father died when he was eleven, and by the time he was seventeen, Williams was a barber in Janesville, Wisconsin. It was there that a local doctor took a liking to the lad and inspired him to embark on a medical career. Williams graduated from the Chicago Medical College in 1883 and opened an office on South Michigan Avenue, where his winning personality, good looks and professionalism attracted many patients, both White and Black. "Dr. Dan," as he became known, was the force behind the founding in 1891 of Provident Hospital, the first Chicago hospital specially for African Americans, although it treated patients of any race. It was at Provident that Williams sewed up a stab wound in a young Black man's heart in 1893—one of the first instances of open-heart surgery on record.

Dr. Dan was just one of the many celebrated physicians in Chicago history. The Danish surgeon Christian Fenger (1840–1902) settled in Chicago in 1877 and introduced the latest techniques from Europe, Nicolas Senn (1844–1908) was the president of the American Surgical Association in the 1890s, Henry Gradle (1855–1911) specialized in germ theory and John Benjamin Murphy (1857–1916) was called "the surgical genius of our generation." Mary Harris Thompson (1829–1895), the founder of the Chicago Hospital for Women and Children, was the first female surgeon in the United States. Bernard Fantus (1874–1940), who was born in Budapest, came with his family to America in 1885, and he received his MD from the College of Physicians and Surgeons in Chicago in 1899. In 1937, Fantus invented and named the blood bank, an innovation without which modern surgery would hardly be possible.

Dr. Fantus created what he first called his "blood preservation laboratory" at Chicago's Cook County Hospital. Established in 1857 as a teaching hospital, in 1916, it moved into a beautiful two-block-long Beaux-Arts building that was designed by Paul Gerhardt. By the mid-twentieth century, it was one of the largest hospitals in the world, with 4,500 beds and 100,000 yearly admissions. As this postcard reveals, it also evolved into one of the world's greatest medical training and research centers. This card was sent by Dr. Abraham Friedman, a specialist in Down's syndrome, to the Institute for Neuropathology in Bonn, Germany, requesting a reprint of a research article. It's not the kind of thing just any hospital could have generated and indicates the depth of the research that was done at Cook County.

By the dawn of the twenty-first century, Cook County Hospital was deteriorating. It closed in 2002 and was replaced by the John J. Stroger Jr. Hospital of Cook County. Yet, the building was too significant to be torn down, so it was converted into a multipurpose facility, containing a hotel, medical offices, a food hall, a daycare center and, fittingly, a museum of the hospital's history. Perhaps the most remarkable aspect of Cook County Hospital was that it took in all patients, no matter how poor or desperate. As Bonnie McDonald, the president of the preservation group Landmarks Illinois once said, "This was really Chicago's Ellis Island....It was where anyone could get service and care at a time where people couldn't afford that healthcare. Anyone could come to Cook County, and they were not turned away."

44

SECOND CITY BROCHURE

Looking at some of the names bordering this 1970s brochure from Chicago's Second City Comedy Theater is like reading a who's who of American comedy in the latter half of the twentieth century—Bill Murray, John Belushi, John Candy, Dan Aykroyd, Gilda Radner, Jerry Stiller, Ann Meara, Eugene Levy, Shelley Berman, Elaine May, Joseph Flaherty, George Wendt, Ed Asner, Alan Arkin, Andrea Martin, Shelley Long, Harold Ramis. And that's not to mention the performers who later joined the troupe, such as Steve Carell, Mike Meyers, Stephen Colbert, Rachel Dratch, Chris Farley, Tina Fey, Valerie Harper, Mike Meyers, Catherine O'Hara, Joan Rivers, Martin Short and Nia Vardalos.

The Second City, which opened on December 16, 1959, defiantly took its name from a snide article in the *New Yorker* on Chicago and its faults by renowned reporter A.J. Liebling. The group had its beginnings at the University of Chicago, where a band of students had formed a kind of club/dramatic society called the University Theater. The mother of one of the group's members, Paul Sills, was the teacher and acting coach Viola Spolin. A pioneer in improvisational theater, she had developed what she called Theater Games, a teaching technique that was initially designed to teach drama to children and immigrants, but which Sills adapted to foster improvisational skills among his university collaborators and to build a modern kind of theater that would more directly involve the audience— to break down the "fourth wall." Sills and his friends first created the Playwrights Theatre Club, which concentrated on mid-century dramas, and

• ROBIN DUKE • TIM KAZURINSKY • EUGENE LEVY • DAN AYKROYD • JIM BELUSHI • JOHN BELUSHI • SHELLEY BERMAN •

ELAINE MAY • ANN MEARA • BRIAN DOYLE-MURRAY • BILL MURRAY • JOSEPH FLAHERTY

JOHN CANDY • ED ASNER • ALAN ARKIN • JACK BURNS • ANDREA MARTIN • SHELLEY LONG

THE SECOND CITY: THE LAUGHS ARE LEGENDARY

SIX CHAIRS ON AN EMPTY STAGE. THE STUFF OF LEGENDS?

Absolutely. The funniest legend in North America. The Second City. From its simple stages have come the BIG NAMES of modern comedy, names like Jim Belushi, Shelley Long, Bill Murray. And in Chicago, Toronto and London, Ontario, you can see the legends of tomorrow. Stars in the making, every night, live. If you like to laugh, and you like the excitement of live theatre, The Second City is just the ticket. Reserve yours today.

FROM THE FRONT PAGE TO THE LIVE STAGE

The undisputed masters of topical satire, the witty writers and brilliant actors of The Second City give us a frank and refreshing view of everyday life. Politics, social and cultural issues, sports, current events; in fact everything in the daily newspaper becomes hysterical show business when The Second City brings it alive. Through scene, song and dance, The Second City delights audiences with the most current and timely references.

DON'T LAUGH. THIS IS SERIOUS THEATRE.

The Second City approach to comedy is no laughing matter. Improvisational comedy is hard work.
Ideas are worked out during the very popular improv portion of the show, ideas which are suggested by you, the audience.
Some of these improvised pieces will be refined, amplified and developed during subsequent rehearsal and will eventually become new material for The Second City shows.
This approach to theatre is completely unique. It is the reason The Second City has the reputation it does for fresh and arresting material.

LOTS OF PEOPLE WANT THE SECOND CITY TO HIT THE ROAD.

The Second City Touring Companies are as popular as the Main Stage troupes. Bringing their humour to schools, college campuses, corporate meetings, theatres and clubs across North America. The touring companies are surefire hits on any road. To book call (312) 664-4032.

GET IN THE ACT

The Second City Training Center offers classes in improvisation for actors. We give the students a chance to study with Second City alumni and to perform on our stage. For information call (312) 664-7952.

THE SECOND CITY. LIVE COMEDY AT ITS ABSOLUTE BEST.

The Second City
The Second City ETC
1616 N. Wells
Chicago, IL 60613
(312) 337-3992

The Second City Northwest
1701 W. Golf Rd.
Rolling Meadows, IL
(312) 806-1555

The Second City ®
CHICAGO

• GILDA RADNER • HAROLD RAMIS • JERRY STILLER • PAUL SAND • DAVID RASCHE • GEORGE WENDT • BETTY THOMAS •

Second City brochure. *Author's collection.*

he then went on to found the Compass Players, what is usually considered America's first improvisatory theater. Working with such talents as Mike Nichols, Elaine May and Shelley Berman, Sills came to appreciate that improvisatory theater could get laughs. Together with fellow University of Chicago alumni actor Howard Alk and director/writer Bernard Sahlins, Sills opened the Second City in a space on North Wells Street that was formerly occupied by Wong Cleaners & Dyers. Sills directed, Sahlins produced and seven performers joined Alk on stage. To their surprise and relief, the first night was a hit. (Audiences sometimes assume everything is ad libbed, but both in the beginning and today, free-wheeling improvisation provided ideas for the skits, which were then constructed and written. Improvisational sketches, however, usually conclude the entertainment.) According to *The Second City: The Essentially Accurate History*, "The first audiences were largely well-educated, well-read young professionals, many of them graduates of the University of Chicago." The performers were not afraid to project a cerebral ambience—this was especially true of Sahlins's productions. One of the early skit characters, for example, was "Dr. Walther von der Wogelweide," the name of a medieval German minnesinger. Soon, celebrities who were passing through town went out of their way to attend, and *Time* magazine called it a "temple of satire." In 1967, Second City moved a few blocks south to its present theater. The Old Town neighborhood was then acquiring a reputation as Chicago's "hippest" area.

In 1961, Second City staged a successful revue in New York; the organization then began sending out other touring companies to different locales, which is still does. Their Toronto gigs were so rewarding that they opened a permanent theater there in 1973. It was in Toronto (Canada's "second city") that the troupe recruited such performers as Aykroyd, Radner, Meyers, O'Hara, Levy, Martin and Candy. In 1974, Toronto and Chicago traded casts for two weeks; the Windy City offering was called *The Canadian Show or Upper USA*. When *Saturday Night Live* came on television in 1975, the producer, Lorne Michaels, happily poached Belushi, Radner and Aykroyd from Second City. Others who followed them to *SNL* included Short, Murray, Meyers, Farley and Dratch. The producers of Second City recognized the obvious: if their performers have TV potential, why not have a Second City TV show? Thus, *Second City Television*, or *SCTV*, which ran from 1976 to 1984, was born, and it gave us such characters as Candy's Johnny La Rue, O'Hara's Lola Heatherton, and Short's illustrious Ed Grimley.

Why did the Second City begin in Chicago and not elsewhere? Since the early twentieth century, Chicago had had an active theater community—the amateur theater at Hull-House and the Chicago Little Theater, for example. But the fact that Spolin had spent most of her very active theater career in the Windy City had much to do with it. Some have argued that performers based in New York and Los Angeles tend to have ambitions for national fame, and although some Second City figures, like Bill Murray, went on to movie stardom, many Chicago actors were (and still are) content to stay local to perfect their skills. And as movie and television production escalated in Chicago, it became easier for homegrown actors to remain in the city. In 2009, a number of Second City alumni gathered in Chicago to mark the troupe's fiftieth anniversary. In an article about the reunion, director Mike Napier told the *Chicago Tribune*, "It always has to be about a show done in the middle of winter in the Midwest. That keeps everything real. That keeps everyone honest." The newspaper, however, pointed out two other key ingredients of success: the ticket prices are low and, "You have always been able to get a drink at your seat."

45

CHICAGO POLICE OFFICER'S RIOT HELMET

I n 1968, the eyes of the world were on Chicago. Normally, that would be welcome, but not in that troubled year. In 1967, Newark, Detroit, Milwaukee and other American cities had endured major race riots, but Chicago, although it had an incident or two, had remained mostly calm. That changed spectacularly after the assassination of Dr. Martin Luther King Jr. on April 4, 1968, when a devastating two-day riot on the West Side left eleven Chicagoans dead, over two thousand arrested and hundreds of buildings burned, all of which was broadcast live on national television. Mayor Richard J. Daley's order to police to "shoot to kill" suspected arsonists drew special undesirable attention.

There was more to come. The Democratic National Convention was scheduled to be held in Chicago in August 1968. This was at the height of the anti–Vietnam War agitation, and demonstrators were planning a massive protest. It was also the apex of the hippie culture, and Chicago, like other major cities, had its own hippie neighborhood, Old Town, which was centered on a funky passageway called Piper's Alley, a kind of counterculture mall with head shops, psychedelic poster galleries and lots of out-of-town sightseers. It was the perfect place for the Yippies, an antiwar group that had been founded in New York on the last day of 1967 with the goal of staging a weeklong "Festival of Life" in Chicago in August to condemn the war and flaunt the hippie ethos, often described as "sex, drugs, rock 'n' roll." The Yippies, whose most prominent figures were Abbie Hoffman, Jerry Rubin and Paul Krassner, were less of a political pressure group and more

Chicago police officer's riot helmet. *Chicago History Museum, ICHi-065719.*

of an antiestablishment street theater, expert in attracting media attention with carnivalesque spectacle. The other major antiwar group headed for Chicago was the National Mobilization to End the War in Vietnam, or "Mobe," a coalition of over one hundred antiwar groups. Mobe, headed by fifty-two-year-old David Dellinger, preached a socialist revolution against racism and imperialism and had little patience with what they saw as the Yippies' childish antics. In 1967, Mobe had held a march on the Pentagon that drew fifty thousand demonstrators and media coverage that brought the antiwar movement into Americans' living rooms, just like the group wanted. Tom Hayden and Rennie Davis, the main organizers of Mobe's activities in Chicago, hoped to attract similar attention in the Windy City.

Mobe's scheme was to mount a giant protest outside the International Amphitheatre, where the Democratic Convention was to be held; they were also organizing events in ten Chicago parks. The Yippies planned a festival of music and theater, in which, Rubin wrote, "New tribes will gather in Chicago. We will be completely open; everything will be free." In March, the Yippies held a "Yip-In" at New York's Grand Central Station. When the crowd got destructive, the police moved in, swinging clubs and breaking heads. It was a publicity coup, but the violence was a portent of Chicago. As author David Farber put it in *Chicago '68*, "The days of the bucolic be-ins was over." As the New York and Chicago Yippies convened in Chicago's Uptown neighborhood, the police began rounding up Piper's Alley hippies on weekends, and police superintendent James Conlisk put a shotgun in every police car, ordered stocks of tear gas and supplied every officer with a riot helmet like this one, which belonged to police officer Max O. Ziegler. The Yippies wanted to hold their protest/festival in Chicago's downtown Grant Park but couldn't get a permit. As Deputy Mayor David Stahl told a Yippie delegation, "Gee, guys, you can't expect the mayor to allow dope and fornication in his front yard." Hoffman warned his followers, "If you're coming to Chicago, be sure to wear some armor in your hair."

The four days of mayhem began on Sunday, August 25. The Yippies assembled in Lincoln Park, conveniently near Old Town. When lingering groups refused to leave at closing time, police ejected them as protestors cried, "Kill the pigs!"—a scenario that was repeated the next two evenings. On Tuesday night, some seven hundred members of the national guard were brought in to assist weary police officers. On Wednesday afternoon, a crowd of nearly ten thousand demonstrators gathered in Grant Park, across from the Hilton Hotel, where many Democratic delegates were staying. Several clashes with police occurred, but things turned violent toward evening, when demonstrators attempted to march down Michigan Avenue to the Amphitheatre. Television cameras rolled as the crowd, chanting,

Police confront protestors on Michigan Avenue during the Democratic Convention, 1968. *Library of Congress.*

"The whole world is watching," was met by a phalanx of police officers who charged into the protestors, swinging night sticks. Tear gas floated above the crumpled bodies of beaten demonstrators as angry police officers herded people into patrol wagons. A federal commission later characterized what became known as the "Battle of Chicago" as a "police riot."

The reaction in the national media was caustic. The *New York Times*, for example, said the violence "brought shame to the city, embarrassment to the country." Historians have since said the Battle of Chicago cemented the growing divide in the United States between the progressives who supported the antiwar movement and the conservatives who sympathized with the police, many of whom were Vietnam War veterans from blue-collar families who considered the demonstrators overprivileged college kids. Between 1932 and 1956, the Democratic National Convention was held in Chicago no fewer than five times. Since the convention of 1968, it has been held there exactly once.

46.

HAROLD WASHINGTON CAMPAIGN BUTTON

Although the symbolic importance of this object is great, its rarity is not. In 1983, they were omnipresent in Chicago. As biographer Roger Biles described it in *Harold Washington: Champion of Race and Reform in Chicago*:

> *Blue Washington campaign buttons appeared everywhere in the African American community, often among city workers who removed the buttons when they went downtown to work in the mornings and replaced them when they returned home in the evenings. Ministers and choir members proudly wore their buttons during Sunday church services.*

In 1983, Chicago was going through a rough spell—city services were deteriorating, city workers were striking, middle-class residents were heading for the suburbs and the tax base was shrinking. The mayor, Jane Byrne, had received the Black community's support in her 1979 election, but African Americans had since come to view her as a practitioner of machine politics who was indifferent to their problems. When Byrne ran for reelection, a challenger with a famous name came forward—Richard M. Daley, the son of Richard J. Daley, also known as "Hizzoner," who had been mayor for twenty years. Only a week later, a third contender emerged—a Black candidate named Harold Washington.

Harold Washington was born in Chicago on April 15, 1922. His father, Roy Washington, had worked himself up from the stockyards to become

Harold Washington campaign button.
Author's collection.

a prominent lawyer and minister. Harold went to DuSable High School and served as a first sergeant during World War II. After the war, he attended Roosevelt College and earned a law degree at Northwestern. Learning from his father, he entered politics—he was a precinct captain in 1954, state representative from 1965 to 1977 and a state senator from 1977 to 1981. In 1980, he was elected to the U.S. Congress; he was reelected in 1982.

Richard J. Daley had received a lot of support from African American voters, but by the 1980s, discontent was rising in the Black community, where the restlessness coalesced around a movement to elect a Black mayor. Washington was reluctant (he had run for mayor in 1977 and had been crushed), but he was finally persuaded. With Byrne and Richard M. Daley splitting the White electorate and boosted by an intense voter registration campaign in the Black wards, Washington won the Democratic primary in 1983 with 36 percent of the vote. Normally, winning the Democratic primary made the victor a shoo-in in the general election, but a great many White voters went over to the Republican candidate, Bernard Epton. The naked racism in some White neighborhoods was appalling, as people wore T-shirts that said, "vote right, vote white," and leaflets warned of rule by "Mr. Baboon" and a city name change to "Chicongo." But the turnout in Black wards was enormous; combined with support from Hispanics and White liberals, it allowed Washington to squeak by with a margin of 46,250 votes out of 1.3 million.

When "Hizzoner" was mayor, no alderman who desired reelection dared vote against him in the city council. That custom abruptly ended under Washington. Of the fifty aldermen, twenty-nine of them, led by "Fast Eddie" Vrdolyak, the chairman of the Cook County Democratic Party (CCDP), and his partner, Ed Burke, formed a majority anti-Washington bloc that stymied the mayor's agenda, resulting in a stalemate that a local satirist nicknamed "Council Wars." Still, Washington managed to pass some reform measures, such as executive orders on freedom of information and affirmative action, a task force on the homeless and a decree banning the hiring and firing of city employees for political reasons. He confronted a serious budget crunch by cutting spending, laying off workers and canceling a property tax cut proposed by Byrne, while Chicago enjoyed an increase in jobs and retail sales.

A breakthrough came in 1986, when the courts ordered a redistricting of ward boundaries to increase minority representation. A special election resulted in the creation of five new Black and Hispanic wards, and the council deadlock was broken—just as Washington's first term was expiring. In the 1987 Democratic primary, he won 54 percent of the votes against a reemergent Jane Byrne; he then won the general election by the same margin. With majority support in the city council, the mayor then believed that the next four years—or more—would allow him to complete his reform agenda. It was not to be. On the morning of November 25, 1987, the mayor suffered a heart attack and died in his office. The outburst of grief, especially in the African American community, was intense.

Under Washington, a dispute took shape that still roils urban politics in America—it might be called "downtown" versus "the neighborhoods." Whereas previous Chicago mayors had boosted development in the business district, Washington encouraged smaller projects in neglected neighborhoods and supported "linked development," in which developers of downtown buildings would pay a fee to be spent in the neighborhoods. After he appointed a committee to report on the issue, one of the members concluded, "Our neighborhoods have suffered long enough, while our tax dollars go to support downtown development." When Chicago's second Black mayor, Lori Lightfoot, was inaugurated in 2019, more than three decades after Washington's death, she said, "We need fairness, which means paying as much attention to our neighborhood business as we do to the businesses downtown. Our neighborhoods have been neglected for too long. They cannot be anymore." The echo of Harold Washington was almost eerie.

47.

CHICAGO BEARS SUPER BOWL SHUFFLE AUDIO CASSETTE

American football fans might argue about which team was the best of all time, but Chicagoans know the answer: the 1985–1986 Chicago Bears. End of discussion.

They were a colorful cast of characters: Jim McMahon, a rebellious gonzo quarterback; Richard Dent, a quarterback-crushing juggernaut who was one of the few defensive players to be named Super Bowl MVP; William Perry, a jolly, gap-toothed lineman who was so huge and unmovable that he was called the "Refrigerator"; two snarling defensive linemen, Dan Hampton, who was known as "Danimal," and Steve McMichael, whose previous team had cut him because they considered him part of the NFL's "criminal element"; Willie Gault, a wide receiver who was so fast that he'd been on a world-record-setting 4x100 relay team; Gary Fencik, a safety from Yale who cut down receivers and running backs like a heat-seeking missile; Mike Singletary, an intense linebacker who was so football-savvy that he was called a "coach on the field" and so lethal that his nickname was "Samurai"; and, of course, Walter Payton, also known as "Sweetness," who was probably the greatest running back in football history. They reminded fans that playing sports was supposed to be fun. They loved Chicago, and Chicago loved them, especially when they did such capers as performing and recording the "Super Bowl Shuffle."

Team owner George Stanley "Papa Bear" Halas was born in Chicago in 1895 and went to the University of Illinois. In 1920, he was hired to coach the Decatur Staleys, a company football team, and he turned it into the Chicago

THE CHICAGO BEARS SHUFFLIN' CREW
THE SUPER BOWL SHUFFLE*

SIDE A
Vocal Mix 5:50
SIDE B
Extended Vocal Mix 6:30
Instrumental Mix 5:30

*A substantial portion of the proceeds from this cassette will be donated to help feed Chicago's neediest families.

Chicago Bears Super Bowl shuffle audio cassette. *Author's collection.*

Bears. He was instrumental in the founding of the National Football League (NFL) and gave it its name. Halas is often thought of as a hard-boiled coach who favored smash-mouth players. That's true, but he was, in the words of Rich Cohen, the author of *Monsters: The 1985 Chicago Bears and the Wild Heart of Football,* "one of the great intellectuals of the game, a brainiac, a football genius." Before Halas, a running back usually took the snap from center and plunged ahead. Halas took the radical step of having the quarterback take the snap and act as a field general, which transformed football into a passing game. Halas's career coaching record was 324–151–31, and before the Super Bowl era, the Bears won eight NFL championships under his leadership. In 1940, the Bears unveiled Halas's perfected T-formation and crushed the Washington Redskins in the title game 73–0 (not a typo). Halas retired in 1968 but returned to the front office at the age of eighty-five to give the Bears two parting gifts. He signed defensive coordinator Buddy Ryan to a three-year contract and then, to everyone's surprise, made forty-two-year-old former Bears tight end Mike Ditka head coach. Ryan and Ditka couldn't stand each other, but they created a superteam.

In the ten games the Bears played at Soldier Field during their Super Bowl season, their opponents averaged 7.4 points. In the playoffs, they held their opponents to 144.7 yards per game and outscored them 91–10. The offense, led by McMahon and Payton, was better than many remember—they led the NFL in rushing yards (2,761) and rushing touchdowns (27)—but the key was Ryan's legendary 46 defense. The "46" didn't refer to any fancy system; it was simply the number worn by bone-shattering safety Doug Plank when Ryan devised the scheme (Plank retired in 1982). If Halas made the quarterback the boss, the 46 was the logical defensive deduction: destroy the quarterback. It was estimated that the opposing quarterback had, at most, three seconds before getting leveled by the Bears defense. But the 46 doesn't work without the right players. With so many defenders rushing, exploitable gaps were left in the secondary; it was a gamble that the defensive line would hit the quarterback before he could find one of those gaps. The Bears' defensive front seven were not just big—they were quick and smart. Ryan also created something called automatic front coverage, in which the defense would analyze the offense's line-up and shift accordingly. At the heart was Singletary, who would size up the situation, call out a code and adjust the defenders' positions. For the opposition, the result was confusion followed by terror.

Sports Illustrated began its report on the 1986 Super Bowl with, "It will be many years before we see anything approaching the vision of Hell that

Chicago inflicted on the poor New England Patriots Sunday in Super Bowl XX. It was near perfect, an exquisite mesh of talent and system, defensive football carried to its highest degree." The Patriots had a total of *seven* rushing yards. Quarterback Tony Eason didn't even complete a single pass. After being sacked three times, he was removed for backup Steve Grogan, who managed a lone touchdown in the fourth quarter. The final score was 46–10.

The winning Bears were the youngest team in the NFL and were figured to win several more Super Bowls. It didn't happen. Analysts have offered several explanations: Ryan left for a head coaching job, the players lost their edge, Ditka pushed them too hard, McMahon got seriously injured and management was too stingy to resign the best players. But the main reason was probably that other teams figured out the 46. They did this by devising the "spread offense," which was developed just to counter the Bears and is now standard practice. Once again, the Bears had changed the way the game is played.

48

MICHAEL JORDAN
CHICAGO BULLS JERSEY

As a lesson in the value of teamwork, it's worth noting that Michael Jordan, most people's choice for the greatest basketball player in history, was in the National Basketball Association (NBA) for six whole years before winning a championship.

Basketball was played in Chicago as early as 1893, especially in YMCAs. The University of Chicago had one of the best college teams, as did Loyola in the 1920s, and the Harlem Globetrotters, despite their name, were founded by Chicagoan Abe Saperstein in 1927. But the professional game was slow in catching on. After the NBA was created in 1949, Chicago endured two failing, short-lived teams (the Stags and the Packers/Zephyrs) before the Bulls became an expansion franchise in 1966. The Bulls made the playoffs in their first year and every year from 1970 to 1975, but they weren't anyone's idea of a powerhouse. Then, in 1984, the Jordan Era began when the Bulls selected the North Carolina star third in the NBA draft (behind Akeem Olajuwon and Sam Bowie).

Jordan was a star from the outset, averaging 28.2 points a game in his rookie year. Although the Bulls annually made the playoffs, they couldn't capture the crown. The Detroit Pistons, the physical "bad boys," knocked the Bulls out of the playoffs three years in a row (1988–1990). But general manager Jerry Krause was building a winning team. In 1985, he signed free agent guard John Paxson, a long-range specialist. In the 1987 draft, Krause landed muscular rebounder Horace Grant and future

Michael Jordan's
Chicago Bulls jersey.
*Collection of John W.
Gustaitis, MD.*

hall-of-famer Scottie Pippen, who became the copilot Jordan needed. In 1988, Krause boldly traded popular forward Charles Oakley for Bill Cartwright, who filled the center position. Not to forget the coaches, in 1989, team owner Jerry Reinsdorf gave assistant coach Phil Jackson the head coaching job. The *Chicago Tribune* said Jackson was, in addition to Reinsdorf, "the only person not fearful of criticizing Michael Jordan." Jackson named Tex Winter, the genius behind the difficult-to-learn "triangle offense," as the offensive coordinator. Once his technique was mastered by Jordan and his associates, it became the secret sauce to the Bulls' six titles.

With everything in place, the Bulls finally defeated the defending champions, the Pistons, trouncing them in four straight games in 1991. After that round, they won their first championship against the Los Angeles

Lakers led by fan favorite Magic Johnson, who said his team had experienced "an old-fashioned butt-kicking." The Bulls won their second championship against the Portland Trail Blazers and their third against the Phoenix Suns. And then, once the "three-peat" was done, Jordan signed to play minor league baseball for the White Sox. He was fairly good, but a baseball strike from August 1994 to April 1995 derailed his plans, and in March 1995, he announced, "I'm back."

Everyone knows the Bulls won six NBA championships, but it's easily forgotten that two different teams won the titles. Only two players—Jordan and Pippen—were on all six of the Bulls' championship squads. After Jordan's two-year break, Krause essentially had to construct a new team around his two all-stars. Many fans and reporters didn't like Krause (he was especially blamed for breaking up the team after the sixth title), but in *If These Walls Could Talk: Chicago Bulls*, sportswriter Kent McDill praised him as "one of the best, hardest-working, and least appreciated general managers in the history of the NBA." Krause signed free agent guards Ron Harper and Steve Kerr, traded for center Luc Longley and, at a time when most general managers were not that keen on European players, signed six-foot-eleven Toni Kukoc of Croatia, who became the Bulls' third-leading scorer. To fill the final slot—a rebounding specialist to replace Horace Grant, who had signed with Orlando—Krause pulled a stunner. He traded for one-time bad boy Dennis Rodman; with his piercings, tattoos and reputation, he was a loose cannon. The "Worm," as he was known, promised to behave, which he did, and his rebounding skills were as promised. A student of the subject, he would watch the opposition practice to see how each player's missed shot ricocheted. The second three-peat came at the expense of, first, the Seattle Supersonics and, in both 1997 and 1998, the Utah Jazz. Fittingly, the winning shot in the 1998 final game was a Jordan jumper with 5.2 seconds left.

Looking back, twenty years later, *Chicago Tribune* sportswriter David Haugh argued that the team's effect on Chicago was long-lasting. Between 1963 and 1986, not a single Chicago sports team won a championship of any kind, and fans were becoming conditioned to expect the worst. The Bulls, he says, "transformed the way a passionate sports town viewed itself, gradually changing the civic psyche from expecting something to go wrong for Chicago's teams to demanding they win it all—or else." In 1994, a statue of Jordan was installed at Chicago's United Center, the Bulls' home stadium. In 1998, after Jordan's second retirement, a quotation from the movie *A River Runs Through It* was inscribed at the base: "At that moment, I knew, surely and clearly, that I was witnessing perfection. He stood before us, suspended above the earth, free from all its laws like a work of art, and I knew, just as surely and clearly, that life is not a work of art, and that the moment could not last."

49.
CLOUD GATE
MILLENNIUM PARK SOUVENIR

Who would have thought in 1999 that the odd-looking object seen here—a blob of something in front of a few buildings— would one day be the kind of thing a tourist would want to bring home from Chicago?

"Pork Place," "Boondoggle Meadow," "Greenback Green," "In-the-Red Square"—these were just *some* of the insults offered by the *Chicago Tribune* in August 2001 as an alternate name for "Millennium Park." In a scalding critique, it griped, "The project has turned into an expensive public-works debacle that can be traced to haphazard planning, design snafus and cronyism." It's true that Chicago's Millennium Park was supposed to cost $150 million and that the final price tag was $475 million. It's also true it was supposed to open in 2000 and that it opened in 2004. But today, Chicagoans and tourists agree that it was worth the wait and worth every dime. With some 25 million visitors a year, it is one of the top tourist destinations not just in Chicago, but in the United States.

The first special attribute of the park is its location—in Chicago's Loop, right on the lakefront. It's miraculous that, at such a late date, a world capital could carve a twenty-four-and-a-half-acre playground out of its core. Second, it redefined what an urban park could be. New York City's Central Park, like others of its era, is a pastoral haven designed to give patrons the illusion that they are far from urban discord. User-friendly Millennium Park is not an escape from the city; it incorporates it and invites visitors to participate in such municipal amenities as concerts,

Cloud Gate Millennium Park souvenir. *Author's collection.*

art and architecture. Finally, both tourists and locals enjoy it, unlike some other attractions (like Navy Pier).

In the 1990s it was a railyard and a parking lot. Planning for the park began in the fall of 1997 and construction began a year later (a 2000 opening *was* optimistic). Edward Uhlir, who had overseen important projects for the Chicago Parks Department, was the supervising architect, and John Bryan, the art-loving CEO of Sara Lee, headed the epic fundraising efforts. The amount of money that came from private donors was practically unprecedented in a public project of this kind. The fact that four of the park's most admired features—the Jay Pritzker Pavilion, the Crown Fountain, the Lurie Garden and the Harris Theater—bear the names of wealthy Chicagoans says volumes about Bryan's ability to woo patrons who were not necessarily eager to back the endeavor, which was fairly vague at the outset. Ultimately, however, the park wouldn't exist without Mayor Richard M. Daley, who put his prestige on the line and weathered the withering criticism. Yes, there were cost overruns but mostly because the evolving plans grew increasingly ambitious and farsighted.

The dominant feature of the park is the Jay Pritzker Music Pavilion, a 120-foot-tall structure with an asymmetric crown of curled stainless-steel ribbons. Facing the stage are four thousand theater seats. Behind them is the Great Lawn, where some seven thousand picnickers can listen to the music through a superb sound system that is supported by an ingenious arching trellis. The architect was Frank Gehry, who was then a hot commodity, having just completed his acclaimed Guggenheim Museum in Bilbao, Spain. Gehry was reluctant to do the project but took it on to please Cindy Pritzker, who, with her husband, Jay, had established the Pritzker Architecture Prize (which Gehry had won in 1989). The Crown Fountain was designed by Catalonian artist Jaume Plensa, who, unlike Gehry, was not an international star at the time, although his work was highly regarded in Europe. Chicago's well-heeled Crown family was not afraid to ask for something innovative. The fountain consists of two illuminated glass brick, fifty-foot towers, on which LED screens display the faces of actual Chicagoans. Jets of water gush from their pursed lips like modern gargoyles. A film of water forms on the large plaza between the towers, providing a popular playground.

As treasured as the pavilion and the fountain are, they haven't become city symbols or trinkets to take home. However, Cloud Gate, also known as the "Bean," a reflective globule of what looks like mercury but is actually made of 168 seamlessly joined plates of stainless steel, has. Designed by Bombay-born British sculptor Anish Kapoor, it was devilishly difficult to engineer, and the complications had to be solved on the fly, which made the costs climb steadily until they reached $20 million (which was donated by corporations and individuals). Though Cloud Gate weighs 110 tons, it looks nearly weightless because it touches the ground at only two relatively small points. The sculpture's luminous reflectivity makes it irresistible to photographers—it is not only seen, it is experienced. According to historian Timothy J. Gilfoyle, the author of *Millennium Park: Creating a Chicago Landmark*, Kapoor said, "Not only do you look at it, it looks at you." The name of the person who came up with the nickname "Bean" is unknown, but the name was applied even before it was finished—even before Kapoor named it Cloud Gate. At first, the artist thought the "Bean" was "completely stupid," which was understandable, considering he had something more cosmic in mind than a legume. But eleven years after the dedication in 2006, Kapoor returned to Chicago and realized the nickname was not malicious but affectionate. He told Hedy Weiss of the *Chicago Sun-Times*, "It's great for it to have a colloquial name, its own lingo. I call it the 'Bean,' too."

50.
CHICAGO CUBS
2016 WORLD SERIES T-SHIRT

Any team can have a bad century."
   To be a fan of the woeful Chicago Cubs baseball team in the latter half of the twentieth century required a sense of humor, and the quip about "a bad century" is a good example of this. Often attributed to Cubs TV broadcaster Jack Brickhouse, the saying seems to have originated with Harvey Walken, a Chicago real estate developer and part-owner of the Pittsburgh Pirates. Another wisecrack came from journalist George Will: "Mamas, don't let your babies grow up to be Cubs fans." And then there was the fan who showed up to the Cubs' opening day with a sign that read, "Wait 'Til Next Year." The team became known as the "lovable losers," a phrase originally applied to the New York Mets, losers of 120 games in 1962. But when the Mets won the World Series in 1969, the Cubs inherited the title. Between 1945, when the Cubs lost the World Series to Detroit, and 2016, they lost 700 more games than they won. And then, in 2016, the unbelievable happened—the Cubs won the World Series. The seventh game of the series ended about a minute after 11:00 p.m. Chicago time, and the T-shirt seen here was on sale the next morning at 10:00 a.m.—a testimony to the craving of Cubs fans for some kind of instant memento.

   In the first half of the twentieth century, the Cubs were one of the most respected ball clubs in the land, winning ten pennants between 1900 and 1945. From 1906 to 1910, the Cubs (World Series winners in 1907 and 1908) compiled a win-loss record of 530–235 (.693), which is still the Major League record for a five-year period. In the 1930s, the Cubs played in the

Chicago Cubs 2016 World Series T-shirt. *Author's collection.*

World Series three times. There were even a few promising seasons after World War II. In 1969, the Cubs' entire infield was on the All-Star team; the Cubs were in first place for 155 days until they lost 17 out of 25 games in a crushing September swoon. The Cubs finished first in their division in 2003, 2007 and 2008, but each pennant quest ended in heartbreak.

Three theories predominated as to why the Cubs were so bad. First, the Cubs were the only team without lights, and a consensus formed that playing in the sun during sizzling Chicago summers wore the players down. Pitcher Rick Sutcliffe once said that, when he pitched at Wrigley Field, he'd lose eight to ten pounds during the game. Second, the management didn't spend money on players because they didn't need to—the fans turned out no matter how crummy the team. In their book *Scorecasting*, Tobias J. Moskowitz and L. Jon Wertheim analyzed the connection between home game attendance and winning records and found that poor performance by the Cubs barely affected ticket sales. About the only thing that did lower attendance, they concluded, was a rise in beer prices. Third, there was the curse of the billy goat. The story says that when William Sianis, the owner of the Billy Goat Tavern (established in 1934), tried to bring his pet goat into Wrigley Field for game four of the 1945 World Series and was refused admittance, he said, "You are going to lose this World Series, and you are never going to win another World Series again." Several attempts were made to remove the curse. Sam Sianis, William's nephew, tried a few times, and in 2008, a Greek Orthodox priest even sprinkled holy water on the dugout—but all to no avail.

As it turned out, it wasn't a priest that was needed—it was a new owner, a new front office and a new manager. And lights were needed, of course, but that was the easy part. The first night game at Wrigley Field was in 1988. The new owner came in 2009, when Tom Ricketts and the wealthy Ricketts family bought the club from the *Chicago Tribune*. Tom Ricketts, a lifelong Cubs fan, took over a mess; Wrigley Field was deteriorating, the minor-league system was the worst in baseball, the front office was computer illiterate, the team's draft choices had been second-rate and the fans were finally getting restless, especially after the South Side White Sox won the World Series in 2005 after enduring their own drought (which was eighty-eight years long). Meanwhile, in Boston, whiz-kid general manager Theo Epstein, who, in 2004, had engineered the ending of a team drought of eighty-six years, had begun to fall out of favor when the Red Sox suffered an epic September collapse in 2011.

When Ricketts heard Epstein might be available, he jumped, and Theo came aboard in October 2011. Three years later, manager Joe Maddon unexpectedly became obtainable when he opted out of his contract with the Tampa Bay Rays. The Cubs made him the highest-paid manager in baseball, and it paid off. Although the Cubs didn't make the playoffs in Maddon's first year, they won ninety-seven games and had developed a solid core of players through smart trades (Jake Arrieta, Aroldis Chapman, Kyle Hendricks, Miguel Montero, Anthony Rizzo, Addison Russell), astute drafts (Kris Bryant, Javy Baez, Kyle Schwarber) and successful free-agent signings (Jon Lester, Dexter Fowler, Jason Hayward, John Lackey, Ben Zobrist). The 2016 World Series, which the Cubs won 4–3, was one for the ages, and many sports analysts called the final game the greatest game seven ever. In Chicago, grown men cried; some went to cemeteries to lay Cubby mementoes on the graves of those who hadn't lived to see the great day. Sportswriter Al Yellon summed it up: "We will never again walk precisely this path, never again (hopefully!) have a drought to bust, never again have to overcome all this history. The dragons have all been slain, every last one of them. We are the champions. It did, in fact, happen."

ABOUT THE AUTHOR

Joseph Gustaitis is a Chicago-based freelance writer and editor. He received his bachelor's degree from Dartmouth College and his master's degree and PhD in history from Columbia University. He is the author of many popular history magazine articles. After working as an editor at *Collier's Year Book*, he became the humanities editor for *Collier's Encyclopedia*. He has also worked in television and won an Emmy Award for writing for ABC-TV's *FYI* program. His previous books are *Chicago's Greatest Year, 1893: The White City and the Birth of a Modern Metropolis* and *Chicago Transformed: World War I and the Windy City*.

Visit us at
www.historypress.com